D1469764

CONSTANTIA UITSIG

THE COOKBOOK

CONSTANTIA UITSIG

THE COOKBOOK

Struik Publishers (Pty) Ltd

(a member of Struik New Holland Publishing (Pty) Ltd)

Cornelis Struik House

80 McKenzie Street

Cape Town 8001

Reg. No.: 54/00965/07

First published in 2000

10 9 8 7 6 5 4 3 2 1

Copyright © in published edition: Struik Publishers (Pty) Ltd 2000

Copyright © in text: Country Lodge Marketing (Pty) Ltd 2000

Copyright © in photographs: as listed below

All rights reserved. No part of this publication may be reproduced, stored in
a retrieval system or transmitted, in any form or by any means, electronic,
mechanical, photocopying, recording or otherwise, without the prior written
permission of the publishers and the copyright holders.

DESIGNER: Petal Palmer

DESIGN ASSISTANTS: Illana Fridkin and Lellyn Creamer

EDITOR: Linda de Villiers

PRINCIPAL PHOTOGRAPHER: Alain Proust

TEXT: Roz Wrottesley and Gail Jennings

Reproduction by Hirt & Carter Cape (Pty)Ltd

Printed and bound by Tien Wah Press (Pte) Limited, Singapore

ISBN 1 86872 445 X

PHOTOGRAPHIC CREDITS

All photographs © Country Lodge Marketing (Pty) Ltd/Alain Proust except
page 6 (© Christiaan); pages 14 centre and bottom left, and 15 (© Food &
Home Entertaining/Jeremy Browne).

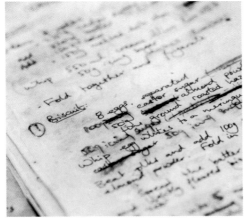

INTRODUCTION

Constantia Uitsig has slipped into the consciousness of Capetonians over the last 10 years as a place for celebrations and special occasions. In a remarkably short time, this working farm has quietly evolved into one of the city's favourite examples of beauty, style and continuity.

For food lovers from all over the world, the combination of sublime setting, imaginative food and world-class service is unforgettable. If they aren't already captivated when they arrive, the Cape works its magic in the time it takes to drink in the serene landscape with a glass or two of Constantia Uitsig Chardonnay Reserve.

Atmosphere is always a hard thing to define, and at Constantia Uitsig it varies from the luxurious buzz of the restaurants to the tranquillity of a shady veranda, from which, if you're lucky, you can watch a family of ducks making their way to the swimming pool for an illicit morning swim.

But wherever you are, there's a soothing sense of harmony, and that speaks volumes for the integrity that underlies the new development. Each building has been renovated or built as it has been needed, and every move has been painstakingly weighed up in terms of history, the future and the welfare of the farm's flora and fauna. An unfailing instinct for detail is what distinguishes Constantia Uitsig from everywhere else. It's visible in the way the new nestles up against the old.

It was always there, the unpretentious farm road lined with vines off the most rustic part of winding Spaanschemat River Road. Constantia Uitsig once belonged to Cape governor Simon van der Stel, as did all of the fertile Constantia Valley. Some things don't change, and two centuries ago the lower slopes of the Constantiaberg were as gentle and accommodating as they are today, and the

Vineyards have flourished at Constantia Uitsig since the 17th century, when Cape governor Simon van der Stel produced his sought-after 'governor's wine'.

breezes from False Bay just as cool. It was here in the first wine-producing region of South Africa that the wines that met with Napoleon's approval were made. The Constantia estate was split up and in 1881 the portion including Constantia Uitsig was bought by farmer Stephanus Petrus Lategan. He and four more generations of Lategans carried on the wine-making tradition without causing so much as a ripple in the world outside their little piece of paradise.

Then, in the late 1980s, there were stirrings: word was that new owners David and Marlene McCay were bringing new ideas to the Constantia Valley's smallest wine estate. More interesting still, they had laid out a cricket pitch with a backdrop of the majestic Constantiaberg, and built a Victorian pavilion in homage to the sport they loved. Magazines rushed in to photograph the phenomenon in all its picturesque detail. Words such as 'taste' and 'style' and 'elegance' were bandied about.

Today there is cricket at Constantia Uitsig every Saturday and Sunday throughout summer. The Constantia Uitsig Cricket Club has a loyal following of fans, but it's also home to the Western

The Constantia Uitsig Cricket Club, with its majestic mountain backdrop, was borne out of passion for the game .

Province Cricket Academy, which trains young cricketers from all over the Western Cape and Boland. At times the youngsters will find themselves taking bowling lessons from the club president and head groundsman, David McCay, a merchant banker and former Western Province swing bowler who still holds the record for the most wickets taken in one match at Newlands: 14 against a Natal B side in 1967.

But competition is not everything at this cricket oval, and Constantia Uitsig's 'English village' matches against visiting teams have become sought-after social events. This is spectator sport at its

most leisurely, styled with white wicker, checked tablecloths and tall glasses of Pimms. It is said that the cricketers themselves don't mind balls going over the boundaries, since they can console themselves with a handful of the grapes that hang so temptingly within reach. Admittedly that might not be true of Pakistani all-rounder Imran Khan, who has played here, and lyricist Tim Rice, who captained an international team.

The exclusive country hotel was the next development at Constantia Uitsig, but for a while it was a secret overseas visitors kept to themselves. It started as accommodation for the cricketers, then

The new has been eased in among the old with infinite care. Architect Michael Doll worked with reverence for the existing organic structure of the property.

grew with the demand from one suite to 16. Before the rest of us realised it was there, its visitors' book was bursting with superlatives, pledges to return, and exotic addresses. We have the loyal overseas visitors to thank for the fact that Constantia Uitsig Restaurant was born to cater for their discerning tastes.

In one of those magical coincidences that Fate seems to bestow on creative people, well-known Johannesburg restaurateur Frank Swainston was looking for a new challenge at just the time when Constantia Uitsig was looking for a top chef. He was reluctant to consider moving to the Cape, but he did come down on holiday ... and drive past the gate ... and, on the spur of the moment, drive in. It was enough. He met the McCays in the driveway and the deal was done.

It was Frank's exquisite food served on the veranda of the manor house before an apron of grass and a semicircle of towering Norfolk pines that put Constantia Uitsig on the map for the local population.

'Uitsig' is 'view' in English, but the Afrikaans word is so much more expressive. The outlook from the relaxed elegance of the restaurant onto the slopes of the Constantiaberg is more panorama or motion picture than mere 'view'. From the restaurant, the valley dips down to a pasture for the horses that are stabled at Constantia Uitsig, and then slopes upwards on the other side to form the screen for an ever-changing spectacle of the seasons. Whatever the weather, the composition of vineyards and oak trees, pine forests and folds of rock is always perfect. The play of light, shade, cloud and mist on the colours of the world below is always breathtaking.

You can't eat Frank's Crespelle di Verdura (page 32) in such a setting without feeling a sense of

'Constantia Uitsig and La Colombe are much more to me than great food in a wonderful setting. When I know I am going to be there I feel happy at the prospect ... The three things I particularly love are the great smells from the kitchens and the gardens, the shining faces that greet you and the great trees which make you lift up your eyes before you lift up that first glass of Constantia Uitsig Chardonnay Reserve.'

Jane Raphaely – *Cosmopolitan* magazine

privilege – no matter how many times you do it. So it seemed almost super-fluous when Uitsig announced the opening of a second restaurant: La Colombe. The chef was a young French-man as dashing as his name: Franck Dangereux. What could he offer that would distract us from the best of the best that was already there?

It is a tribute to Marlene McCay's instinct and Franck's inspiration that, three years on, La Colombe thrives. Franck's food is passionately, authentic-lly, extravagantly French. It's not the kind of food you indulge in every day, but once you've tasted it, there are times when nothing less will do. He cooks from the heart here, he says, as he has

OPPOSITE: *Frank Swainston's wizardry in the kitchen quickly established Uitsig as a little piece of heaven for discerning diners.*

LEFT: *Franck Dangereux is inspired at La Colombe – 'my little restaurant among the vineyards' – as he has been nowhere else in the world.*

'There are cooks, there are chefs and there are creators of exquisite sensual experiences. At its best Frank's food produces a shock of pleasure. Deep layers of flavour, textures and aromas entwine, leaving a seductive memory that you want to recapture again and again. Our regular Sunday lunches at Franck's La Colombe Restaurant are an indulgence that always restores the spirit and cossets the senses in every way. Long may it continue.'

Mica and Marina Naumann

done in few other places he's been to in the world. The sense of peaceful industry at Uitsig, the tranquillity and the availability of fresh produce have made his 'small restaurant among the vineyards' a constant revelation.

His domain was once the farm's pool room. A reverent refurbishment transformed it into an inspiring space by the addition of a lofty pitched ceiling and pastel paintwork. Mornings on the veranda and around the pool are beautiful beyond belief and breakfast is served here for hotel guests. The squirrels love it and have become quite adept at helping themselves to their share of the scones.

There has always been a vision for Uitsig, but Marlene is a conservationist, so there have never been any of the tyrannies of profit goals and time lines and marketing objectives. The vineyards have their seasons, but for everything but the winemaking there are no development deadlines to keep to.

So, until recently, the entrance to the farm was marked by an old school house, unused for years and patiently awaiting its fate. The idea for a roadside coffee shop and deli came from chefs/caterers Judy Badenhorst and Graham Isaacson. Judy had a special interest in the place: she and André Badenhorst, Uitsig's wine maker, were the last people to live in the manor house before it became the restaurant. Before that they lived on a neighbouring farm and Judy created one of Constantia's favourite institutions, the original Old Cape Farm Stall in Spaanschemat River Road.

The Spaanschemat River Café opened in October 1999 and was an instant, almost overwhelming success. The battle to keep up with demand has done nothing to dampen Judy and Graham's delight in catering to a clientele who appreciate their adventurous flavour combinations and gorgeous presentation. Coffee shop it can be, if you want it, but it's also a restaurant of rare sophistication.

There are no extravagant signboards proclaiming the presence of Constantia Uitsig and Marlene McCay likes it that way. It would have been easy to respond to the grandeur of the surroundings by creating something impressive and imposing, but understatement – which serves the estate so well – starts at the gate. The River Café announces itself discreetly to passing motorists, but most people take the drive intentionally, allowing it to feed their anticipation and their appetites.

In the Cape, appetite means wine, and winemaking is a low-key but vital function of the farm, supervised with almost religious passion by wine director André Badenhorst. When he joined the McCays at Constantia Uitsig a decade ago, he set the farm's centuries-old grape-growing tradition on a new course for the future. After a thorough analysis of soil, weather, topography and slope, he embarked on an eight-year uprooting and replanting programme.

OPPOSITE: *Wherever they go on the estate, people feel the same sense of seclusion, peace and tranquillity.*
ABOVE: *Judy Badenhorst and Graham Isaacson's Spaanschemat River Café opened in November 1999. Within days, there was hardly a seat to spare.*

Instead of Cape Riesling, Chenin Blanc and Cinsaut, Constantia Uitsig now produces Chardonnay, Sauvignon Blanc, Sémillon and Merlot, alongside the existing Cabernet Sauvignon – all noble cultivars ideally suited to the climate in the valley. The first 750 cases of Constantia Uitsig Dry White, made from Sauvignon Blanc grapes, emerged in 1993. With 30 hectares under vine, Constantia Uitsig is the smallest of the Constantia Valley wine estates, producing 17 000 cases of wine a year.

The Constantia Uitsig Chardonnay Reserve is the most acclaimed of all the wines: the '97 vintage won a Veritas Double Gold award and is one of the chosen few on the South African Airways winelist. The Sémillon Reserve, the Merlot and the Cabernet/Merlot blend have all been award winners too. Together with the excellent Cabernet Sauvignon, Sauvignon Blanc and popular Uitsig Blanc (a blend of Sémillon, Chardonnay and Sauvignon Blanc that has earned the right to be the house wine at the restaurants), they're available at the Constantia Uitsig Wine Boutique, over which André presides, next to the River Café.

A wine cellar is part of the vision for Constantia Uitsig, but like everything else, it will come when the time is right. And when it does, it will have that 'there forever' feeling that makes the estate so special.

BELOW: *An eight-year uprooting and replanting programme has set the centuries-old vineyards on course for the future.*

OPPOSITE: *Seven years after the first new Constantia Uitsig wine was bottled, the estate's Wine Boutique boasts seven wines and many awards.*

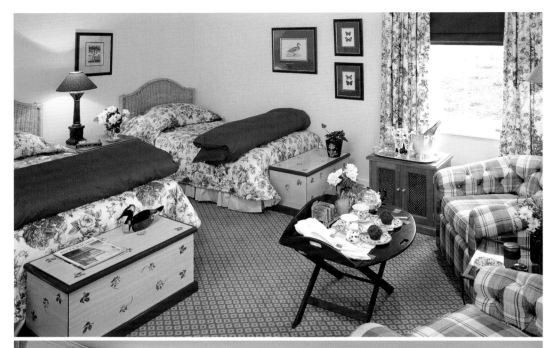

Accommodation originally designed for one visiting cricket team has expanded to a 16-suite country hotel that's a haven for international travellers. Guests don't just stay – they form a relationship that brings them back time and time again.

This bliss is in the detail: fluffy white towels and gowns, roses freshly picked from the garden, desks that encourage written reflection, porcelain and wood, deep drapes, snug chairs and generous eider-downs. These are rooms that are hard to leave.

'The old adage tells us that "location is everything". Well, not quite everything at Constantia Uitsig. There is also ambience, manifested in "establishment" Cape Dutch décor and architecture, memorable dining experiences via innovative dishes and fine wines, and discreet, informed service. The view – yes, it's stunning – but so is everything else that creates the character of this unique restaurant. Constantia Uitsig is high on the list of my favourite dining experiences.'

Colin Sharp – *Habitat* magazine

Frank's foie gras at Constantia Uitsig Restaurant

has been described as

'É come un sogno con gli occhi aperti.'

('It's like a dream with your eyes open.')

OPPOSITE: *There's a visual feast in every glance, harmony in every angle.*

Frank Swainston

If chef Frank Swainston can't be found in Uitsig's kitchen, he's probably beaming a warm welcome in the smart reception area, glass of wine in hand. Or settled at one of the tables, talking with guests – listen for his easy, infectious laugh. For Frank is not merely a renowned chef – 'I'd rather be known as a cook' – he's a consummate host.

English-born Frank honed his people-skills as a waiter, barman, salesman, croupier and casino manager; he spent a miserable few months as a sous chef, then decided that 'self-taught' – plus a little help from travels in Italy – was how he'd rather be. He opened his first restaurant, Trattoria Fiorentina, in January 1976 in Johannesburg, followed by Frank's Trattoria Italiana 12 years later. 'Working as a chef is certainly not a "job",' says Frank. 'It's a way of life, and you can't do it unless you love it. I like being under pressure, and love seeing the immediate results – joy and satisfaction – of my work.'

Franck Dangereux

At 15 Franck Dangereux enrolled at the Hotel School in Nice where, as one of the top five students, he was rewarded with further training under three-star Michelin chefs Roger Vergé (at his Moulin de Mougins) and Louis Outhier (at L'Oasis la Napoule).

In 1994, after a stint in St Barthélemy in the French West Indies, 20-something Franck arrived in South Africa to visit his uncle. He met Frank Swainston by chance a week later and next thing was his sous chef – Franck's line of persuasion may not work in every profession, though: 'I want to feel that drop of sweat falling off my nose!'

Itchy feet took him to the rest of Africa for a year or so, but on his return he felt the need to cook once more. The result? One small corner of Constantia Uitsig that is forever Provence.

La Colombe's (The Dove) menu – written up in French on a blackboard and translated, like poetry, by the waiting staff – changes every day, depending on what's available. The food is always sensual, stylish, distinctly French. 'I use local ingredients, cooked the French way.' says Franck.

'Whenever I want to celebrate,
whenever I need cheering up
The last meal before I leave town, the first when I return,
Always La Colombe.
Simply, sublimely, superbly the best.'

Theo Otten

Judy Badenhorst and Graham Isaacson

Judy Badenhorst and Graham Isaacson have worked together for the last 10 years or so – they started the first Old Cape Farmstall – and all the while, they've been on the lookout for the perfect site – a free-standing venue for a fine-food café and deli.

From the moment it opened in October 1999, Judy Badenhorst and Graham Isaacson's 'café' has had hardly a rattan seat to spare. It's the third gastronomical success story on the farm, with the same easy-going formula: great service, excellent food and the right people to pull it all together.

Judy can't remember a time when she didn't nurture a passion for good food. 'I love the creative power of cooking: who decides what flavours go with what? I do! I've even found myself in the kitchen at 3 am, making ice-cream. I'd woken up and just known that's what I had to do right then.'

Graham claims he's more the business side of their ventures, but Judy insists that his creativity and intuitive sense of flavours are a constant inspiration.

CONSTANTIA UITSIG

'Cooking is about giving.

There is no magic needed,

it only requires love and care.

My greatest joy lies in cooking for

my family and friends ...

to me this is really "cooking with love!"'

Frank Swainston

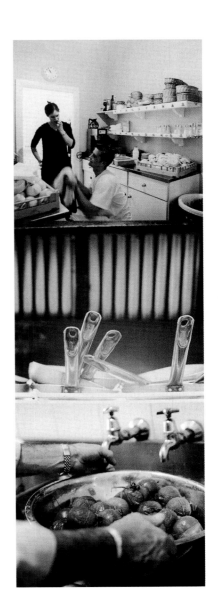

'I love pasta or fresh vegetables in season

for starters. So, of course, fresh vegetable pasta

is my favourite.'

CAPONATA

'This is a dish I love very much, and it's a favourite among vegetarians. It's Sicilian, and has been on the menu for years – we make it when we can get really good celery and aubergines.

'Caponata needs excellent vinegar, so don't skimp on quality – usually, expensive equals good!' At Uitsig, when we get the chance, we make our own vinegar – it's something we should do more often, as we have all these vineyards.'

1 kg aubergines, washed and unpeeled

salt

olive oil for frying

1 large bunch white celery, cleaned and cut into short lengths

1 large onion, sliced

1 small tin tomato paste, diluted with a little warm water

salt and freshly ground black pepper to taste

20 ml sugar

red wine vinegar to taste

30 ml capers

20 green olives, stoned

plenty of freshly chopped flat-leaf parsley

Dice the aubergines. Sprinkle with salt and leave to drain in a colander for 30 minutes. Wipe dry, then deep-fry in hot olive oil until brown. Drain on paper towels.

Fry the celery in the same oil.

In a clean pan, sauté the onion until golden. Stir in the tomato paste. Season and cook for 15 minutes over moderate heat. Stir in the sugar, vinegar, capers, olives, aubergines and celery.

Add the parsley and leave to get cold. Serve on bruschetta, rubbed with a little garlic. It can also be served on pasta – just add a little more tomato. SERVES 6 OR MORE

WINE SUGGESTION: Uitsig Cabernet Merlot or a light red wine

RISOTTO WITH SPARKLING WINE AND SAFFRON

'A few years ago at Uitsig we devised a menu to celebrate our Constantia Valley. I used sparkling wine from the farm next door, Buitenverwachting, in this dish – just for the joy of it. Drink the rest of the bottle with your meal – or, if you can't wait, while you're cooking.

'People often ask me for the secret to risotto. There isn't one – just buy good rice (I like Riso Gallo's Carnaroli) and keep your eye on the pot. For this risotto, buy the best saffron you can find – there are a lot of fakes out there – because there's nothing to beat the flavour and colour of the real thing.'

1.5 litres chicken stock (If you're going to serve the risotto with fish, use fish stock.)
200 g butter
50 ml olive oil
1 medium onion, chopped
50 ml sparkling wine
400 g Italian risotto rice (There's no need to rinse it first – I only ever rinse Basmati rice.)
saffron soaked in a little stock
salt and freshly ground black pepper to taste
Parmesan cheese (I like Padanno Regiano)
a small glass of sparkling wine

Heat the chicken stock.

In another pan, warm 50 g of the butter and the olive oil. Gently fry the onion until it's soft – about 15 minutes. Add the 50 ml sparkling wine, then add the rice and stir until it's coated in butter and wine.

Add 2 ladlefuls of boiling chicken stock, just enough to cover the rice. Simmer, stirring continuously, until the rice has absorbed nearly all the liquid. Add the soaked saffron.

Continue to add more stock until most of it has been absorbed. (To keep you going, start on the sparkling wine!) The rice will eventually be creamy and *al dente*. Taste for seasoning.

Add the rest of the butter, the Parmesan and sparkling wine. Stir carefully, so it doesn't become stodgy.

Cover and let it stand for 10 minutes off the heat. Serve on its own as a starter, or as an accompaniment to meat or fish. SERVES 6

WINE SUGGESTION: The same sparkling wine that you used in the risotto

CRESPELLE DI VERDURA

(ROULADE OF PANCAKES

LAYERED WITH A MOUSSELINE OF VEGETABLES ON A FRESH TOMATO AND BASIL SAUCE)

PANCAKES

3 fresh eggs

200 ml milk

70 g flour

10 ml olive oil

salt to taste

olive oil for frying

FILLING

1 kg leeks, white part only, sliced

butter for frying

salt and freshly ground black

pepper to taste

1 kg Swiss chard

500 g ricotta

a pinch of grated nutmeg

1 kg pumpkin, peeled and cubed

Parmesan for topping

To make the pancakes, combine all the ingredients, except the olive oil for frying, and whisk together. Let the mixture rest for at least 1 hour.

Heat a 30 cm frying pan, then add a very thin layer of olive oil (pour off most of it). Pour in enough batter to make the first of three pancakes, making sure the mixture is evenly distributed around the pan. When you see small bubbles, turn the pancake over. Fry until golden. Remove from pan and make the next one. This mixture makes quite a rubbery pancake, as it must act as a container for the filling.

To make the filling, open the leeks and wash them very well to clean them. Dry thoroughly, then chop. Fry in butter, with salt and peppr, until butter is absorbed. Purée the leeks and set aside.

Blanch the Swiss chard and dry thoroughly. Chop finely and fry in butter until butter is absorbed and Swiss chard is 'dry'. Add the ricotta cheese, nutmeg, salt and pepper. Set aside.

Roast the pumpkin, then purée and season it.

On a board, spread leek purée over one pancake. Place another pancake on top, and spread with the Swiss chard purée. Repeat the procedure with the pumpkin purée.

Roll up and wrap tightly in foil. Refrigerate overnight.

Slice into eight pancake rolls. Dot with butter, sprinkle with Parmesan and grill until golden and hot inside. Place on a bed of tomato and basil sauce (see page 149). SERVES 8

WINE SUGGESTION: Rosé or a Blanc de Noir

'A few years back, Giambiero Geminiani, the chef/patron of Solferino

in Lucca, visited South Africa for an Italian Week in Johannesburg,

hosted by the Italian government. We cooked together for

that week, and he gave me this recipe.

It's been on the menu ever since we opened.'

SPICY THAI SOUP

'This is one of the recipes that has come to me during the last two years or so.

I visited Australia and came back with all these wonderful tastes.

It's proof that I've been influenced by the times!

'At Uitsig we use Three Chefs Tom Yum paste – it's imported from Thailand,

but you'll find it at any good supermarket, deli or speciality store.'

12 black tiger prawns, peeled with
heads and shells reserved
30 ml peanut oil
2 litres chicken or fish stock
3 lime leaves
12 button mushrooms, sliced
15 ml grated fresh ginger
1 bunch spring onions
30 ml Tom Yum paste
butter for frying
salt and freshly ground black
pepper to taste
1 tin coconut milk
45 ml chopped fresh coriander
30 ml Thai fish sauce
45 ml fresh lime or lemon juice
1 packet Chinese noodles

In a large pan, sauté the prawn shells with the heads in the peanut oil for about 5 minutes, stirring all the time. Pour in the stock with the lime leaves. Simmer for 15 minutes.

In a separate pan, fry the mushrooms, ginger and onions and mix in the Tom Yum paste. Strain the stock from the shells. Add to the mushroom mixture and bring to the boil.

In a small frying pan, fry the prawns in a little butter. Season with salt and pepper. When the prawns are almost cooked, add them to the soup. To finish, add the coconut milk, coriander, fish sauce and lime or lemon juice.

Cook the noodles according to the packet instructions. Divide into four soup bowls, and pour the soup over. SERVES 4

WINE SUGGESTION: Gewürztraminer or an off-dry white

ROCKET SALAD
(A SALAD OF ROCKET, MIXED GREENS, TOMATOES, BACON, CROUTONS AND A POACHED EGG)

'This peppery, vibrant salad has been on the

menu ever since we opened our doors.

It's so popular – people never seem to tire

of rocket and fresh greens.'

1 packet mixed salad leaves
120 g rocket
75 ml crispy cubed bacon
4 slices bread, cut into cubes and
fried in butter
4 smallish tomatoes, skinned
and diced
4 eggs, lightly poached
1 x recipe Frank's vinaigrette (see
page 154)

Mix all ingredients, except the eggs and vinaigrette, together in a bowl. Drizzle
with vinaigrette. Divide among four plates and top each serving with an egg.
SERVES 4

WINE SUGGESTION: Uitsig Blanc

CAESAR SALAD

'There are Caesar salads and there are Caesar salads! This way – the New York way –

is how I think it should be made, and I've made it like this for 40 years!

'It's not necessary to use only Romaine lettuce (Cos). If you can't find enough,

mix the Cos with Iceberg – it'll still be wonderful.

The anchovy mayonnaise is also delicious with cold poached chicken or cold veal.'

300 ml home-made mayonnaise (see page 154) (If you'd rather use prepared mayonnaise, use a good brand.)

5 cloves garlic, peeled and chopped

18 Sicilian or Spanish anchovy fillets (They're sometimes difficult to find, but always worth the hunt.)

a few bacon rashers, fried and cut into small squares (optional)

5 cloves garlic, peeled and halved

olive oil for frying

ordinary sliced white bread, cut into cubes

salt and freshly ground black pepper to taste

very good Parmesan cheese, grated

3 firm Romaine lettuces, washed and dried

Place mayonnaise, chopped garlic and 10 of the anchovy fillets in a blender and process until smooth. Spoon into a bowl and set aside.

Chop the remaining anchovy fillets and fold into the mayonnaise. (Add the bacon, if using.) If the mayonnaise is too thick, add a drop or two of water.

Fry the halved garlic cloves in olive oil until light brown, then add the bread cubes and fry until golden brown. Drain on paper towel. Discard the garlic and season the bread cubes. While they're still hot, sprinkle with some of the Parmesan.

Tear the lettuces into large pieces and place in a salad bowl. Toss with the mayonnaise and sprinkle with the remaining Parmesan. Scatter the croutons over and serve. SERVES 6

WINE SUGGESTION: Uitsig Blanc

SPAGHETTI ALLA GENOVESE

(SPAGHETTI WITH PESTO SAUCE, NEW POTATOES AND BABY GREEN BEANS)

'As the waiting staff explain to anyone who orders this spaghetti, it's my favourite pasta dish. I first tasted the traditional Genovese combination when I was 19 and spent a year in Italy washing plates and working behind the bar.

'At the restaurant we use small new potatoes, but you can use older potatoes – just cube them. Make sure you buy good quality spaghetti – at Uitsig we use Del Verde or Da Cecco, both imported from Italy and available from most supermarkets.'

12 new potatoes
250 g green beans, cut in half
500 g spaghetti
200 g pesto sauce (see page 154)

Cut the new potatoes in half and place in a large pot with plenty of salted water. Bring to the boil, add the green beans and cook for 2 minutes. Add the spaghetti and cook until *al dente* – about 12 minutes.

Drain and place the spaghetti, potatoes and beans in a heated bowl. Add the pesto. If necessary, thin the sauce with a little water from the spaghetti pot, or with extra olive oil. SERVES 6

WINE SUGGESTION: Uitsig Blanc

SPAGHETTI VIAREGGINA

(SPAGHETTI WITH CLAMS AND TOMATOES)

2 x 240 g tins baby clams
3 cloves garlic, finely chopped
1 small onion, finely chopped
olive oil for frying
125 ml dry white wine
500 g ripe tomatoes, peeled,
seeded and chopped (or a tin of
plum tomatoes)
1 red chilli or to taste
salt to taste
500 g spaghetti
freshly chopped parsley
freshly ground black pepper

Drain juice from the tins of clams and set aside. Sauté the garlic and onion in olive oil until soft. Add the wine and cook until reduced by half. Add the tomatoes and the clam juice. Season to taste with the chilli and salt. Cook over a brisk heat for 15 minutes.

Cook the spaghetti in plenty of boiling, salted water until just tender.

Meanwhile, add the clams and parsley to the tomato sauce, season and leave for a minute for the clams to absorb the flavours.

Drain the spaghetti as soon as it is cooked. Dress with the hot sauce. SERVES 6

WINE SUGGESTION: The white wine you used for cooking

'This is one of the most beautiful pastas, with a rich, concentrated flavour.

I first met it in the '60s, when I visited Viareggio. My wife is from this region

of Italy, and you can find fresh clams, beautiful tomatoes, lots of olive oil ...

'If you can buy fresh clams, good (don't forget to soak them to get rid

of the sand); if not, Mayfair and John West make excellent tinned clams.'

CARPACCIO DI PESCE

(THINLY SLICED RAW FISH WITH A SOY SAUCE,
RED WINE VINEGAR, SESAME SEED OIL, GINGER AND SEAWEED DRESSING)

'I love raw fish – and I love ginger (especially tea with ginger and cardamom) –
so this is a perfect combination.

'Don't be afraid to prepare raw fish. It takes a lot of time, but it's worth it.
You will need a sharp knife, and use whatever very fresh fish is available –
Cape salmon, salmon trout, kabeljou, yellowfin tuna or yellowtail, but never hake.'

500 g very fresh white fish, with all
the blood and bones removed
500 g very fresh salmon trout or
salmon
1 x 20 cm square of nori seaweed
fresh coriander to garnish
DRESSING
60 ml soy sauce (At the restaurant
we use Kikkoman's.)
30 ml red wine vinegar
30 ml sesame oil
15 ml grated fresh ginger
5 ml wasabi paste (Japanese
horseradish paste)

Roll the fillets of fish in plastic wrap and place in the freezer.

Mix together all the dressing ingredients and leave to stand.

Cut the nori into 8 x 7 mm-wide strips. Soak the strips in the dressing.

Take the fish from the freezer and unwrap. Slice it as thinly as possible. Arrange the pink fish in the centre of the plate and the white fish around it until the whole plate is covered.

Dress with 30 ml of dressing. Arrange the nori over the fish and sprinkle with chopped, fresh coriander. SERVES 8

WINE SUGGESTION: Rosé

ICED PLUM TOMATO SOUP
WITH MOZZARELLA AND BASIL OIL

**'I discovered this wonderful fresh soup at The Ivy, one of London's most popular restaurants –
it's almost impossible to get a table, but it's worth any wait.'**

500 g very ripe tomatoes, halved
and seeded
500 g cherry tomatoes
300 ml good quality tomato juice
45 ml balsamic vinegar
2 cloves garlic, peeled and finely
chopped
salt and freshly ground black
pepper to taste
TO GARNISH
small mozzarella balls (3 per plate
for soup)
basil leaves
mixed cocktail tomatoes – cherry,
plum, yellow and red
olive oil for drizzling

Process all the tomatoes in a blender with the tomato juice, balsamic vinegar and garlic. Pass the mixture through a fine sieve, then check the seasoning (remember that cold dishes need much more seasoning than usual). Chill the soup in the freezer for 30 minutes.

Serve in very cold soup plates with mozzarella balls, some basil leaves, halved cherry and plum tomatoes and a good drizzle of olive oil. (Add a few droplets of basil dressing – basil leaves steeped in olive oil and then blended.) SERVES 6

WINE SUGGESTION: A fresh young white wine

FETTUCCINE AL PEPE

(RIBBON NOODLES WITH NEAPOLITAN TOMATO SAUCE AND PESTO WITH CREAM)

'Lucca was again my source of inspiration for this pasta.

A friend owns a restaurant there, and he gave me the recipe.

I've served it to him at Uitsig,

and he was quite happy with my variations.'

1 kg ripe or tinned tomatoes

4 cloves garlic

50 ml olive oil

1 large onion, finely chopped

1 large carrot, finely chopped

1 stalk celery, finely chopped

1 bunch fresh basil, finely chopped

salt and freshly ground black
pepper to taste

1 x recipe pesto sauce (see
page 154)

a dash of cream

a little Parmesan

700 g fettuccine

If you're using fresh tomatoes, peel and chop, discarding the seeds (the seeds make the sauce more acidic). Crush the garlic cloves with the blade of a knife.

Heat the oil in a deep pan and sauté the garlic until brown. Discard the garlic, saving the oil. Add the finely chopped vegetables, chopped herbs, tomatoes and salt and pepper to taste. Simmer for 1 hour over moderate heat.

Mix in the pesto sauce with the tomato sauce, add a little cream and grated Parmesan. Cook the pasta in plenty of salted water until *al dente*, then drain and toss with the sauce. SERVES 6

WINE SUGGESTION: Rosé or Constantia Uitsig Sauvignon Blanc

VINE TOMATOES BRAISED IN OLIVE OIL

'Beautiful. I love them.

Tomatoes must be red and ripe – to get their full beauty

they must have their stalks on. Good food stands on its own.

The tomatoes in the photograph were devoured by the

photographer and me, with our freshly baked bread hot

from the oven. Try this dish with a grilled fillet steak or veal.'

180 ml olive oil
8 cloves garlic, peeled
a handful fresh basil, chopped
6 sprigs fresh thyme
6 large red vine tomatoes, peeled
sea salt and freshly ground black
pepper to taste
castor sugar

Put the olive oil, garlic and herbs in a heavy, flame-proof casserole over low heat and cook until the garlic begins to soften.

Add the tomatoes stem-side down, and sprinkle with salt, pepper and a pinch of sugar. Cover and cook very gently for 8 minutes, then turn carefully and sprinkle with salt, pepper and a pinch of sugar.

Cover and cook very gently for 10 minutes more, or until tender when pierced with a skewer, basting occasionally with the oil.

Eat hot or cold with good bread. SERVES 6

WINE SUGGESTION: Rosé or Constantia Uitsig Sauvignon Blanc

BEEF CARPACCIO CON RUCOLA

(THINLY SLICED RAW BEEF WITH ROCKET, VINAIGRETTE AND SHAVINGS OF PARMESAN)

'This dish was invented by Arrigo Cipriani of Harry's Bar
in Venice, where they serve it with a liquid mayonnaise
and sliced celery dressing.

'It's particularly popular at Uitsig, where it is sometimes served
with avocado.'

500 g whole beef fillet
salt and freshly ground black
pepper to taste
rocket leaves
1 x recipe Frank's vinaigrette (see
page 154)
shavings of Parmesan Regano (not
the ground, supermarket fare)

Wrap the fillet tightly in plastic wrap. Place in the freezer, along with the
serving plates.

When the fillet is semi-frozen, take it (and the plates) out and slice very
thinly. Cover the centre of each serving plate with slightly overlapping slices.
Season to taste.

In a salad bowl, mix the rocket with the vinaigrette. Toss to cover. Arrange
the rocket leaves with Parmesan shavings in the centre of the plate. SERVES 6

WINE SUGGESTION: Uitsig Sémillon Reserve

'I like simple food, prepared with thought, love and care.

That's our secret at Constantia Uitsig.'

FILLET OF SOLE FIORENTINA

**'This dish has been on my restaurant menus since the
summer of 1976 – and will always be. I love it.'**

6 x 300 g soles, filleted into
4 pieces each (keep the head,
bones and skin for stock)
salt and white pepper to taste
500 g frozen spinach (or 5 bunches
Swiss chard, washed well and
with the stems removed)
a little butter
300 g button mushrooms, sliced
1 clove garlic, peeled and
finely chopped
15 ml freshly grated Parmesan
STOCK
head, bones and skin of 6 soles
2 onions, roughly chopped
12 parsley stems
30 ml lemon juice
250 ml dry white wine
100 fresh mushroom stems
SAUCE
60 ml butter
75 ml plain flour
a little cream

First make the stock. Place all the ingredients in a saucepan and cover with cold water. Bring to a simmer, then skim off the top. Simmer uncovered for 30 minutes. Strain and set aside.

Arrange the sole fillets in a roasting pan and season lightly. Pour in the hot stock and leave for a minute, then drain the poaching liquid into a new dish. Cover with buttered paper and set aside.

Defrost the spinach just enough so that you can cut it with a heavy knife. Cut it into small pieces. Melt a little butter in a saucepan, then add the spinach and season. Cover and cook very slowly until the spinach has thawed, then uncover and raise the heat. Cook until all the moisture has evaporated. (If using Swiss chard, place in a large pot of salted water. Boil uncovered for 5 minutes. Strain and plunge into ice water to preserve the colour. In small handfuls, squeeze out as much liquid as possible.)

To make the sauce, melt the butter. Blend in the flour and cook slowly, stirring until they foam and froth together without colouring. Take the saucepan off the heat, and beat in the boiling fish stock. Keep stirring until the sauce thickens. Add a little cream.

Preheat oven to 200 °C.

Fry the mushrooms and garlic in a little butter until dry. Mix with the spinach and a little of the sauce and Parmesan. Divide the mixture between six gratin dishes. Place 4 sole fillets on top, then a little of the sauce and a little more Parmesan. Cook in the oven for 10 minutes, then place under the grill to brown. Serve hot. SERVES 6

WINE SUGGESTION: Constantia Uitsig Sauvignon Blanc or Chardonnay

NORWEGIAN SALMON
WITH CREAMY SPARKLING WINE SAUCE

4 x 220 g salmon

2 large potatoes, diced into

1-cm cubes

4 leeks, chopped in large pieces

1 vanilla pod

water or wine

salt and freshly ground

black pepper to taste

tomatoes, cubed

spring onions, chopped

SAUCE

250 ml cream

150 ml sparkling wine

100 ml fish stock

50 ml butter

salt and white pepper to taste

First make the sauce by reducing the cream, sparkling wine and fish stock by two thirds (or until the sauce resembles molten lava). Blend the sauce in a blender, adding the butter. Season with salt and white pepper.

Place the potatoes, leeks and vanilla pod in a roasting tray with a little water or wine, salt and pepper. Cover with foil and place in a 200 °C oven for 15–20 minutes, or until the potatoes are tender.

Season the salmon with salt and pepper. Heat a dash of oil in a hot pan and sear the salmon for 1–2 minutes on each side, making sure not to over cook. Put the salmon in a 200 °C oven for a further 2 minutes.

Divide the potatoes and leeks among four large plates, top with sauce and a portion of salmon. Surround the salmon with the fresh tomato and spring onions and serve with deep-fried sweet potatoes. SERVES 4

WINE SUGGESTION: Buitenverwachting Cap Classique Brut

'This is simply stunning. If you can't get springbok,

other venison will do, and it's always cooked rare. In his book

Cape on a Plate, South African food writer Tony Jackman voted this

one of the top 10 dishes in the country.'

LOIN OF SPRINGBOK
WITH LEMON AND HONEY SAUCE

2 onions, finely chopped

50 g butter

300 ml honey

100 ml lemon juice (or to taste)

150 ml dark beef and veal stock

(see page 148)

salt and freshly ground black

pepper to taste

2 x 700 g loins of springbok

olive oil for frying

Caramelize the onions in butter and honey. Add the lemon juice. Pour in the stock and cook for 30 minutes, then strain through a fine sieve into a small saucepan and cook for a further 30 minutes. Season and add more butter to make the sauce shine. Set aside.

Season the springbok with freshly ground black pepper and salt. Sear in a very hot pan with a little oil to make a crust. Do not overcook – 5 minutes is enough, as it must be rare.

Pour a little sauce on each plate. Slice the springbok into medallions. Fan out and place on the sauce. Serve with stir-fried vegetables.

SERVES 4

WINE SUGGESTION: A good red

MAGRET DE CANARD
WITH MALAGASY PEPPERCORN SAUCE

'A favourite on the menu since we opened. It's simple and quick –
nowadays you can buy vacuum-sealed duck breast in some
supermarkets. It's a very meaty dish, and must be rare –
although many people think duck should be well-done.

'The sauce is particularly versatile – we also serve it with fillet steak
or medallions of tuna.'

6 duck breasts
SAUCE
6 spring onions, chopped
100 g green peppercorns, crushed
(reserve some whole
peppercorns for garnish)
5 ml English mustard (We use good
old Colemans.)
100 g butter
dash of brandy
250 ml white wine
500 ml meat stock (see page 148)
250 ml cream
salt to taste

In a saucepan, cook the spring onions, peppercorns and mustard in the butter.
Deglaze with the brandy and white wine. Add stock and cream, and reduce by
half. Take off heat and blend. Add the whole peppercorns and check seasoning.

Slash the skin of the duck breasts diagonally, just down to the flesh. Cook, skin-
side down, in a hot frying pan large enough to hold them all at the same time –
they must not touch each other, otherwise they will boil and not fry. Watch that
they do not burn – 10 minutes, until the skin is golden, should be enough. Turn,
and cook for another 4 minutes on the other side.

Pour a little sauce onto each plate. Slice each breast into about eight slices and
fan on top of sauce. SERVES 6

WINE SUGGESTION: Klein Constantia Rhine Riesling

GRILLED SALMON TROUT FILLETS
WITH WHOLE GRAIN MUSTARD SAUCE

'We use fillets fresh from Three Streams in Franschhoek, so this is a thoroughly local dish.'

1 litre good fish stock (made with the bones of the salmon trout)
1 bunch spring onions, finely chopped
200 g butter
250 g mushrooms, finely chopped
225 ml Noilly Prat or dry Vermouth
250 ml cream
dash of lemon juice
60 ml whole grain mustard
salt and freshly ground black pepper to taste
4 x 200 g salmon trout fillets
butter for frying

Boil the fish stock until it has reduced by half.

Cook the onions in a little butter until soft, then add the mushrooms and the Noilly Prat. Boil for 10 minutes and strain.

Mix the cream, lemon juice and mustard into the stock, then whisk in the remaining butter. Season.

Grill or fry the fillets in a little butter.

Spoon the sauce onto fish platters and place the fish on top of sauce. Serve with new baby potatoes. SERVES 4

WINE SUGGESTION: Klein Constantia Rhine Riesling

TRIPPA ALLA FIORENTINA

(TRIPE COOKED THE FLORENTINE WAY)

1.3 kg ox tripe

2 large onions, chopped

1 bunch celery, roughly chopped

4 carrots, scraped and chopped

3 bay leaves

200 ml olive oil

½ head garlic, peeled and chopped

15 ml each finely chopped
fresh rosemary, parsley and basil

2 large onions, chopped

1 bunch celery, sliced into 2 cm-
lengths, leaves discarded

4 carrots, scraped and sliced

3 x 420 g tins peeled Italian
tomatoes, chopped

salt and freshly ground black
pepper to taste

freshly grated Parmesan for serving

Boil the ox tripe until cooked (about 2 hours) in plenty of salted water with the onions, celery, carrots and bay leaves. Leave to cool in the stock.

When cool, take out the tripe and cut into slices. Remove any excess fat from the stock, then set aside, in case you need it later.

In a large pot, heat the olive oil. Add the garlic and herbs. Stir. Then add the onions, celery and carrots and brown slightly.

Add the cut tripe. Cook, stirring, for 15 minutes, then add the tomatoes with the juice. Season and cook slowly for about 2 hours. If it starts to dry out, add some of the stock from the tripe pot. Serve with grated Parmesan. SERVES 6

WINE SUGGESTION: Uitsig Sémillon

'Boiled tripe in sandwiches is the national dish of Florence – it's street food. I've always loved tripe.

I served it at my first restaurant, in Johannesburg, and when I arrived in the kitchen at Uitsig, of course

I put it on the menu. It didn't take off right away, but then word began to spread – word of mouth,

so to speak. Now we sell about 50 kg a week. And Dave (McCay) loves it!

'No matter how anyone may shudder, I'm passionate about tripe! My mother used to make it with

onions, milk and flour. I like it boiled and sliced with raw onions and lots of parsley.

Even my children love it – I've never had to force them to eat it!'

ABBACCHIO ALLA TOSCANA
(SLOW-ROASTED SHOULDER OF LAMB WITH ROSEMARY AND GARLIC)

'The succulence of slow-roasted meats, particularly lamb, is a sensation like nothing else.

Started in a cool oven, these meats are exactly what I mean by simple

food, well prepared with care.'

LAMB

1.5 kg forequarter racks (ask your
butcher to divide them
into portions)

6 sprigs fresh rosemary

6 cloves garlic, chopped

salt and freshly ground black
pepper to taste

150 ml extra virgin olive oil

SPINACI ALLA GENOVESE

(SPINACH WITH RAISINS

AND ALMONDS)

2 kg fresh spinach, washed,
trimmed and cut into small pieces

100 g butter

100 g raisins, soaked in warm
water for 15 minutes

100 g sliced almonds

salt to taste

Place the lamb racks in a roasting pan with the rosemary and garlic. Season. Pour over the olive oil and put into a cold oven. Set the oven to 140 °C and slow roast for 3 hours, turning them halfway through the cooking time.

To make the spinach, steam for 5 minutes until half cooked. Drain carefully and squeeze out any remaining water with your hands.

Melt the butter in a large pan, add the spinach and mix together using two forks. Drain the raisins and add to the spinach, followed by the almonds. Mix, then season to taste.

Serve at once with the lamb and roasted potatoes. SERVES 6

WINE SUGGESTION: Uitsig Cabernet Merlot

WILD DUCK

3 x 1.4 kg wild duck
salt and freshly ground black
pepper to taste
olive oil
6 stalks celery, finely chopped
6 medium-sized carrots, finely
chopped
4 large onions, finely chopped
300 g streaky bacon, cubed
1 small bunch fresh thyme
4 bay leaves
5 ml juniper berries, crushed
strong meat stock (see page 148),
to cover the duck
750 ml good red wine
30 ml corn starch, thinned with a
little of the red wine or water
50 g dried wild mushrooms (such
as porcini), soaked in warm water
500 g fresh brown
mushrooms, sliced
butter for frying
6 cloves garlic, peeled and
finely chopped
a handful fresh parsley (without the
stalks), chopped

Preheat the oven to 250 °C.

Trim the ducks of all fat and chop off the wing points. Season. Rub ducks with olive oil and place in the oven. Roast for about 20 minutes, until golden brown. Allow to cool, then cut in half and remove the backbone.

Brown the vegetables with the bacon and herbs. Add the roasted ducks and juniper berries to the pan and cover with the stock and wine. Bring to the boil. Lower the heat to a simmer and simmer for 1–1½ hours (or until cooked – check them. If you're using ordinary duck, they'll probably need only 1 hour).

Remove the ducks from the liquid. Reduce the liquid by half, then thicken with the corn starch.

Fry the dried and fresh mushrooms in butter with the garlic and parsley, and add to the thickened sauce. Return the ducks to the sauce and heat through. Serve with sliced polenta and vegetable cake (see page 71) or with spring onion mash.
SERVES 6

WINE SUGGESTION: The same wine you used in the dish, or a lovely Shiraz

'This is our biggest selling dish, and I've been making it for years.

I think it's wonderful – I love casseroles and stews.

'We get our wild ducks from a farm in Johannesburg – they're small, dark and

delicious. They can also be tough and strong tasting, so they have to cook for quite

some time in order to absorb the flavours well. If you can't find wild duck,

use ordinary duck, but don't cook it for as long.'

LINE FISH SERVED
WITH CRISPY CABBAGE AND ORIENTAL SAUCE

'At Uitsig we only serve fish that's been caught on the day. Our deliveries arrive at 11 am, and we take whatever is the freshest. So we can never be sure what'll be on the menu.

'Why the combination with cabbage? I love cabbage – it has a wonderful texture, which contrasts so well with its accompaniment: sweet potato. And, of course, cabbage and oriental flavours are perfect together.'

fillets of fresh white linefish –
kabeljou, kingklip, Cape salmon
(about 220 g per person)
1 x recipe Frank's spicy Oriental
sauce (see page 151)
CRISPY CABBAGE
½ medium-sized cabbage
150 ml sesame oil
100 g icing sugar
50 ml dry sherry
15 ml grated fresh ginger
1 red chili, chopped
120 ml white wine vinegar
100 g sultanas, soaked in water
salt and freshly ground black
pepper to taste

Break up the cabbage into individual leaves – remove all thick stems and cut the leaves very finely. Sprinkle with salt. Cover and leave in the refrigerator overnight. Wash thoroughly and drain well.

Heat the sesame oil in a large pan and add cabbage for a minute, coating all leaves. Push the cabbage to one side. Add the icing sugar. Cook until it starts to caramelize. Stir in the cabbage again and mix. Add the sherry, ginger, chilli, vinegar and sultanas. Cook over high heat for 5 minutes or until all the liquid has evaporated – the cabbage should be golden and slightly crispy. Cool and adjust seasoning.

Season the fillets and cook in a very hot pan with a little sesame oil. (Depending on the thickness of the fish, it should cook for about 3 minutes each side.) Do not overcook.

To serve, place the cabbage in the centre of the serving plate. Set the fish on top of the cabbage and surround with Oriental sauce. Top with deep-fried, finely sliced sweet potato and fresh coriander. SERVES 6

WINE SUGGESTION: Uitsig Chardonnay

SPICY PRAWNS
AND NOODLES WITH JULIENNE OF VEGETABLES

'I simply love eastern flavours: chilli, oyster sauce, ginger ...

The fragrance is captivating. What more can I say?'

32 king-size tiger prawns

butter for frying

30 ml oyster sauce

5 ml chopped garlic

5 ml chopped fresh ginger

chopped fresh red chilli to taste

dash of mirren (Japanese
rice wine)

dash of white wine

½ tin coconut milk

handful coriander sprigs, chopped

1 small bunch fresh basil

1 bunch spring onions, chopped

300 g egg noodles or
linguini/spaghettini

JULIENNE OF VEGETABLES

1 large carrot

2 courgettes

4 yellow patty pans

6–8 mangetout

florets of broccoli

Blanch all the vegetables, separately, in boiling salted water – about 4 minutes each. Remove and place into ice-cold water to stop the cooking. Place all the vegetables in a strainer.

Lightly fry the prawns in butter. Add oyster sauce, garlic, ginger and chilli. Coat the prawns with the sauce. Deglaze the pan with the mirren and white wine.

Add the coconut milk and cook until it thickens. Take it off the heat and add the coriander, basil and spring onions.

In the meantime, cook the noodles or pasta according to the packet instructions. Mix in the heated vegetables. Divide between four soup plates and pour over the prawns and sauce. SERVES 4

WINE SUGGESTION: Uitsig Sauvignon Blanc

POLENTA AND VEGETABLE CAKE

'The colours in this polenta cake are so beautiful –

when it's sliced through it looks like a slab of marble.

'Eat it with Gorgonzola, tomato, wild duck, stews, casseroles,

or simply on its own. It's as heavenly as it looks.'

100 g broccoli florets
100 g carrots, sliced
100 g cauliflower florets
100 g courgettes, sliced
500 g instant Italian polenta
salt and freshly ground black
pepper to taste
knob of butter
100 g Parmesan, grated
olive oil for frying

Blanch all vegetables, separately, in boiling salted water – about 4 minutes each. Remove and place in ice-cold water to stop the cooking. Place all the vegetables in a strainer.

Make your polenta as directed on the packet – it should take about 5 minutes.

Using a wooden spoon, mix in the vegetables. Season. Add the butter and the Parmesan.

Line a loaf tin with foil and pour in the polenta and vegetables. Flatten the top with a palette knife and leave for 1 hour in the refrigerator. Remove from the foil and slice, then fry in a little olive oil.

Serve when slightly browned and hot. SERVES 6

WINE SUGGESTION: Constantia Uitsig Sauvignon Blanc

'I could probably do without dessert, but I'm here to make

my guests happy! The grilled peaches and poached pears

are my favourites, although all our desserts are sensual,

elegant and delicious.'

FROZEN NOUGAT WITH A KIWI FRUIT SAUCE

'Sometimes this is on the menu, sometimes not. So you'll have to take your chances –

or make it at home. It'll keep for quite some weeks in the freezer.'

600 g icing sugar

500 ml honey

125 ml light corn syrup

sugar thermometer

8 egg whites

2 litres cream

600 g golden raisins, soaked
in water

250 g candied red cherries,
chopped

125 g candied orange peel,
chopped

600 g assorted dried fruit

375 g shelled walnuts

250 g roasted almonds

KIWI FRUIT SAUCE

4 kiwi fruit, peeled (you can use
apricots, peaches or
nectarines, too)

250 ml sugar

juice of 2 lemons

Mix together the sugar, honey and syrup in a non-reactive saucepan. Put the sugar thermometer in the saucepan and heat the mixture until it reaches 120 °C.

In a large bowl, whisk the egg whites until soft peaks form. Add the hot syrup in a thin stream and whisk until cool.

Add the cream, beating until incorporated.

Fold in all the fruit and nuts – the mixture will be quite stiff. Pour the nougat into an oiled bread tin. Cover with foil and freeze overnight, then slice.

To make the sauce, cook the ingredients, blend together and then cool.

SERVES UP TO 15

MARQUISE AU CHOCOLAT

'This is the ultimate rich chocolate dessert – some of our regular guests at Uitsig have never even tried any of our other desserts: they pick this one every time.'

145 g dark chocolate, melted
12 egg yolks, beaten
250 g castor sugar
45 ml granulated coffee, dissolved in 60 ml water
100 g clear honey
300 g unsalted butter
165 g cocoa powder
500 ml double-thick cream
orange crème Anglaise (see page 153)
melted chocolate for garnish

Mix melted chocolate into egg yolks, castor sugar, coffee and honey.

Melt 15 ml of the butter and grease the loaf tin. Line with plastic wrap.

Beat the remainder of the butter and cocoa together and stir into the egg mixture.

Whip cream into soft peaks and fold into the mixture, using a metal spoon. Pour into a loaf tin and refrigerate for 24 hours.

To serve, pour crème Anglaise into the serving plate. Pipe circles of melted chocolate over, then drag a toothpick from the centre through the lines to the edge of the plate or from the plate edge to the centre. Use a hot knife to unmould the chocolate and place slices or scoops in the centre of the crème anglaise. SERVES 6

ROBBIE'S BREAD AND BUTTER PUDDING

'In my trattoria in Johannesburg, the same people would come in every day to eat. We had no menus, but would write up the daily fare on a board. One customer, Robbie Robinson, would always ask for bread and butter pudding, but I never got around to making it.

'Better late than never, though. Once at Uitsig, I discovered a recipe I liked and made a pudding – then forgot about it and left it in the refrigerator until the next day. Ever since, I've served it cold with cream – it's delicious. And Robbie made it down to Cape Town – and approved of my innovation.'

60 g unsalted butter
8 soft bread rolls, thinly sliced
50 g sultanas, soaked in whisky
and drained
600 ml milk
600 ml cream
2 vanilla pods, split
6 large, fresh eggs
300 g castor sugar
apricot jam
runny cream for serving

Grease an oval pie dish with a little of the butter.

Butter the rolls with the remaining butter and arrange the slices in the base of the dish. Sprinkle over the drained sultanas.

Place milk, cream and vanilla pods in a pot and bring to the boil. Whisk together the eggs and castor sugar. Add the milk and cream mixture to the egg mixture, beating continuously.

Preheat the oven to 220 °C.

Strain the mixture over the bread and leave to soak for at least 1 hour – or longer.

Place the dish in a *bain-marie* and pour in enough hot water to reach halfway up the dish. Poach carefully in the oven for 50 minutes. Remove and allow to stand until cold. Brush on melted apricot jam and leave in the refrigerator for at least 3 hours.

Serve cold with cream. SERVES 6

POACHED PEARS IN RED WINE

(WITH CINNAMON AND STAR ANISE AND ROLLED IN ROASTED HAZELNUTS)

'While we're poaching the pears, the scent of the simmering fruit and spices is bewitching – it permeates the whole of the kitchen and restaurant.'

4 sticks cinnamon
6 star anise
zest of 1 lemon
zest of 1 orange
750 ml good red wine
500 ml castor sugar
1 vanilla pod, split
6 large pears, peeled with the stalks still on
250 g ground roasted hazelnuts

Place all the ingredients, except the hazelnuts, in a saucepan, bring to the boil and simmer for about 1 hour or until the pears are soft. Remove cooked pears with a slotted spoon and leave to cool.

Reduce the spiced wine by half over a high heat to the consistency of syrup. Strain.

Roll the pears in the ground hazelnuts, stand upright on plates and pour over the syrup. Serve with crème fraîche. SERVES 6

'Cooking is probably the only ephemeral art where creations are meant to be eaten and savoured. It is a craft of the heart that opens wide the window of the senses and sometimes even touches the soul.'

Franck Dangereux

'The starter is my best part of the meal. It takes the edge

off your initial ravenousness, and often it is the most enjoyed dish

of them all. Sometimes I hide behind the window at La Colombe

and watch. I love to see the expressions on guests' faces

as they first discover the flavours.'

LE PAN BAGNA DE L'AMI BRUNO

(BRUNO'S SOAKED BREAD)

'I've named this sandwich after my childhood friends Bruno and Stephane. They were some of my early "victims" – they would have to try out whatever I cooked. We loved to eat this dish. The old Provençal version was made from left over stale bread soaked in olive oil and tomato pulp. Now every sandwich shop and deli in Provence sells them, with lettuce, tomato, cucumber, tons of vinegar and olive oil. You can't possibly eat it in a clean way: you have to eat in on the beach, then go for a swim, to wash off the olive oil dripping down your chin.

'I've "civilized" the *pan bagna* a little and put it on a plate, so guests at La Colombe don't have to dive into the swimming pool after their meal.'

2 eggs
1 small loaf of pain campaillou (see page 156)
or 1 ciabbata, sliced 1-cm thick
1 clove garlic
1 punnet cherry tomatoes
1 small jar calamata olives
1 x recipe paletta sauce (see page 151)
olive oil
balsamic vinegar
10 basil leaves, finely sliced
1 bunch chives, snipped
1 bunch spring onions, chopped
1 packet mesclun (see page 90) or
mixed salad leaves
8 Italian, French or Spanish anchovy fillets (for good anchovies you have to spend money)

Boil the eggs for 6 minutes, then refresh in cool water to prevent further cooking. Peel and cut in half.

Toast the bread under the grill on one side only. When it's cool, scratch the toasted surface with the garlic clove. Set aside.

Slice the cherry tomatoes in half.

Place a slice of bread in the centre of each plate. Arrange the tomatoes and olives around the bread and pour paletta sauce (tomato pulp) over each slice of bread. Pour olive oil over the sauce and drizzle over a few drops of balsamic vinegar.

Sprinkle the herbs and spring onion on the plates.

Dress the salad leaves in a little olive oil and balsamic vinegar and place the leaves carefully on top of the bread. Top with the eggs and anchovies. SERVES 4

WINE SUGGESTION: Sauvignon Blanc or a dry rosé

TARTARE DE THON FRAIS À LA CORIANDRE ET AU SOJA

(FRESH TUNA TARTARE WITH RED ONION SALAD)

'I discovered raw fish when I was sailing in the Caribbean.
Every day, unless the sea was rough, we'd put out a line for tuna.
Then big or small, we'd slice it thinly and devour it, with a squeeze
of lime and a dash of soy sauce and olive oil. Those were the most
wonderful of meals.

'If you can't find the freshest of tuna or dorado, you can substitute
with yellowtail. The red onion salad must be prepared the day before.'

RED ONION SALAD
2 medium red onions, thinly sliced
15 ml chopped fresh coriander
60 ml fresh lime juice
60 ml olive oil
salt and freshly ground black
pepper to taste
TARTARE
480 g filleted, skinned fresh tuna
2 tomatoes, skinned, seeded
and diced
45 ml thinly sliced spring onion
30 ml finely chopped fresh
coriander
60 ml olive oil
salt and freshly ground black
pepper to taste
60 ml freshly squeezed lime juice
olive oil and soy sauce for serving
30 ml snipped chives to garnish

Make the salad the day before it's required by combining all the ingredients.
Stir well, cover and refrigerate.

Dice the tuna into 5 mm cubes.

In a large mixing bowl combine all the ingredients, except the lime juice. Mix
well to coat. Add the lime juice just before serving and mix well.

Spread a little red onion salad in the centre of six serving plates. Using an egg
ring, divide the tuna mixture among the plates. Drizzle a little olive oil around
each tartare, then a few drops soy sauce, and garnish with the chives. SERVES 6

WINE SUGGESTION: A crisp, dry Sauvignon Blanc

'A "tian" is actually the name of a clay dish in which vegetables are cooked in Provence.

The result is always vegetables that melt in the mouth, with all the flavours harmonizing with one

another. A tian has now become the name of a dish that has these same flavour qualities.

'I have made tons of tian in my life – it's another of those apprenticeship nightmares,

where you have to make them perfectly in a metal mould.

For this dish you'll still need a mould, but you don't need to do it perfectly.'

TIAN DE TOMATE, AUBERGINE ET D'AVOCAT AU BASILIC, GROSSES CREVETTES ET VINAIGRETTE DOUCE AU CHILLI

(TIAN OF AVOCADO AND AUBERGINE WITH BASIL, LARGE PRAWNS AND SWEET CHILLI SAUCE)

2 large ripe tomatoes

olive oil for frying

salt and freshly ground black pepper to taste

1 large aubergine, cut into four thick rings (drain and salt the aubergines if they are not in season or if they are not completely ripe)

2 ripe avocados

10 basil leaves, coarsely chopped

juice of ½ lemon

20 large prawns, peeled and heads removed

a metal cookie cutter/ring mould the same size as the tomato slices

1 x recipe sweet chilli sauce (see page 150)

1 x recipe basil dressing (see page 155)

snipped chives to garnish

Slice a little off the top and the bottom of each tomato, then cut each one in half, horizontally (as if along the equator). Fry the four tomato slices in olive oil until browned – the tomato must be cooked through but not puréed. Season on both sides with salt and pepper.

Do the same with the aubergine. It will need more oil and will take longer to cook, but don't make the oil as hot. Drain on absorbent paper towel and season.

Half the avocados and peel – pull off the skin carefully. Cut into large cubes. Place in a mixing bowl with the basil, lemon juice, salt and pepper and a splash of olive oil. Stir gently with your hands – if you use a spoon you'll ruin the avocado. Place it in the refrigerator.

Season and fry the prawns in olive oil until browned. Don't overcook, though – no more than 2 minutes.

To assemble: Place the cutter or ring mould in the middle of the plate. Wedge in the tomato slice, making sure it touches the edges. Add a layer of the avocado mix, then an aubergine slice. Finish off with more avocado. Put five prawns on top of each tian. Carefully remove the cutter or ring mould. Drizzle a little olive oil on top of and around the tian. Then drizzle with sweet chilli dressing and a few drops of basil dressing. Garnish with freshly snipped chives. SERVES 4

WINE SUGGESTION: Blanc Fumé, Sauvignon Blanc or wooded Chardonnay

LA SALADE DE CAILLE 'DES BADENHORST'

(JUDY AND ANDRÉ'S QUAIL SALAD)

4 quails

5 quail eggs (just in case one
doesn't turn out quite right)

STOCK

the quail carcasses

olive oil

1 small onion, chopped

1 small carrot, chopped

1 small stalk celery, chopped

2 cloves garlic, coarsely chopped

50 ml balsamic vinegar

100 ml white wine

1 litre cold water

DRESSING

the concentrated stock

15 ml Dijon mustard

30 ml balsamic vinegar

50 ml sunflower oil

20 ml sesame oil

salt and freshly ground

black pepper to taste

SALAD

2 Golden Delicious apples

butter for frying

40 green grapes (or thereabouts)

1 packet mesclun (mixed leaves)

olive oil

balsamic vinegar

Ask your butcher to take the fillets or breasts off the bone and to take the legs off the carcass and remove the femur.

To make the stock, chop up the carcasses. In a large saucepan, heat a little olive oil to sizzling point. Add the carcasses and caramelize. Add the vegetables and cook until they are brown. Deglaze with the vinegar and wine, cook for 3 minutes, then add the cold water. Cook on medium heat until reduced by three-quarters. Strain through a fine sieve, return to a saucepan and reduce until it almost starts to thicken. This will be a very concentrated stock – you'll end up with about half a cup. Do not add salt, as the reduction will make the salt even more concentrated.

While the reduced stock is still warm, make the dressing. Whisk in the mustard and vinegar and gradually add both oils. Season to taste.

To make the salad, peel the apples and scoop the flesh into balls with a Parisian scoop (like a melon baller). Fry in butter until golden brown. Slice the bottom off each grape to give it an even surface on which to balance.

Season and fry the quail legs until brown – it will take about 2 minutes on each side. Then fry the breasts – this will take only 1 minute on the skin side and 30 seconds on the meat side. Be careful not to overcook, as the meat is so delicate. Set aside.

Soft poach (40 seconds) the quail eggs in red wine.

To assemble, dress the mixed leaves in a little olive oil and a few drops of balsamic vinegar. Heap the leaves in the centre of each plate. Place the apples and the grapes in a circle around the perimeter of the plate, alternating apples and grapes. Slice the breasts thinly and arrange around the salad. Place the two legs on top of the salad and drizzle with the dressing. Put the quail eggs on top of the legs. SERVES 4

WINE SUGGESTION: Rhine Riesling or a Gewürztraminer

'I like it when someone does the hard work for me, so in this recipe we do the hard work

for our guests: deboning the quails!

'Quail deboning is a typical practical test set at French hotel schools – you have to do it from the inside,

so the bird remains whole. Not a favourite task.

'I created this dish especially for Judy and André Badenhorst back in 1994.'

PETIT RAGOÛT DE SUPIONS ET CREVETTES AU BASILIC ET AU PIMENT

(RAGOUT WITH PRAWNS, CALAMARI, BASIL AND CHILLI)

4 squares of 7 cm x 1 cm thick puff
pastry (see page 157)
15 ml water
1 egg yolk
200 g small calamari tubes,
cleaned
12 tiger prawns
oil for frying
15 ml chopped garlic
15 ml chopped chilli
30 ml chopped fresh basil
RAGOUT SAUCE
4 medium-ripe tomatoes, peeled
½ medium onion
60 ml red wine vinegar
100 ml olive oil
salt and freshly ground black
pepper to taste
HERB BUTTER
50 ml cream
15 ml Dijon mustard
30 ml lemon juice
150 g butter
1 small bunch each chives, chervil,
tarragon and parsley

First make the ragout sauce. Combine the tomatoes, onion and vinegar in a blender and blend to a fine pulp. Add the olive oil and season with salt and pepper. Set aside.

Place the cream for the herb butter in a small saucepan with the mustard and lemon juice and reduce by half. Then whisk in the butter until melted. Season and take off the heat. Keep warm. Wash the herbs, drain and chop them finely. Add to the warm sauce (a hot sauce will cause the herbs to turn grey).

Preheat the oven to 200 °C. Place the puff pastry squares on a baking tray.

Add the water to the egg yolk and brush the top of each square with the egg wash. Bake for 15–20 minutes.

When the squares are slightly cool, use a bread knife to slice the squares horizontally to separate the bases from the tops.

To assemble, slice the calamari into small rings and peel the prawns. Warm a large frying pan on high heat and add a splash of olive oil. When the oil is hot, add the prawns and calamari. Cook for 30 seconds, then add the garlic and chilli and cook for another 30 seconds.

Deglaze with the ragout sauce and cook, uncovered, for 2 minutes. Add the basil.

Place the puff pastry bases onto the plates and divide the ragout between the four plates. Pour a swirl of herb butter onto each ragout. Place the lids on top and serve. SERVES 4

WINE SUGGESTION: Constantia Uitsig Chardonnay Reserve 98

'This dish was inspired by my experiences in Morocco. I learned about cooking prawns and calamari from the fishermen there. They'd sear prawns with rock salt on a thick piece of metal, then peel them and eat them just like that. Or they'd fry baby calamari in lots of olive oil, chilli, garlic and tomato pulp and eat them with bread. Seeing them cook was like discovering good, simple food all over again.'

MESCLUN DE LANIÈRES
DE CALAMAR AU PIMENT ET AU CITRON

(SPICY CALAMARI WITH MESCLUN)

olive oil for frying

400 g tenderized calamari steak,
sliced into 1-cm strips

20 ml crushed garlic

15 ml chopped fresh ginger

15 ml finely chopped fresh chilli

1 packet mesclun or mixed
salad leaves

30 ml chopped spring onions

SAUCE

100 ml lemon juice

300 ml dry white wine

100 ml oyster sauce

First make the sauce. Combine all the ingredients and set aside.

In a large frying pan, heat the oil until sizzling. Fry the calamari strips until they begin to brown on the edges. Add the garlic, ginger and chilli. Fry gently for 1 minute. Deglaze with the sauce and cook until reduced by a third.

To serve, divide mesclun into four and pile onto four plates. Spoon the calamari next to the leaves. Drizzle the rest of the sauce over the leaves. Garnish with the spring onion. SERVES 4

WINE SUGGESTION: A wooded Chardonnay or an Auxerrois

'For me there are only two ways to prepare calamari –

stuffed and slow cooked for a very long time or flash fried.

'I used to make this recipe with soy sauce and sugar.

One day I decided to make it at home, but had neither ingredient.

So this dish with oyster sauce was born by accident.

'Mesclun is Provençal dialect for "mix". At La Colombe we make

mesclun with 12 different salad leaves: butter lettuce, lollo rosso,

lollo bionda, baby cos, rocket, watercress, mazuma, mibuna

(almost like mustard leaf), oakleaf lettuce, salad burnett, chervil,

sometimes basil, baby spinach (tatsoi). A bag of assorted leaves from a

good food store will do just fine.'

TARTE FINE
AUX AUBERGINES, ONIONS ET GORGONZOLA

'This is a variant of one of the most delicious things on earth – a pissaladière: fried onions, fresh thyme, olives, anchovies, on top of a crisp dough baked in a wood oven. Every bakery in Provence makes them. I used to buy one every day on my way to school. 'For this dish I use puff pastry and bake it in a conventional oven. You can use just about any ingredients – peppers, spinach, fennel ... If you use tomatoes, bake them first.'

1 large onion, peeled and thinly sliced
olive oil
1 sprig thyme
500 g aubergines
salt and freshly ground black pepper to taste
300 g puff pastry (see page 157)
(Puff pastry is wonderful to make, but if don't have the time, buy a good brand at a supermarket.)
150 g Gorgonzola
1 tot Grappa
1 egg

Fry the onion in olive oil until brown and 'melted'. Add the sprig of thyme and set aside. Thinly slice the aubergines, horizontally or vertically. (You only need to salt aubergines if they're old, and you shouldn't be using old aubergines!) Fry in olive oil and reserve on absorbent paper. Season after cooking.

On a floured surface, roll out the puff pastry 3 mm thick. Cut out 4 saucer-sized pieces and place them on an ungreased baking tray. Use a fork to prick the middle of the pasty, leaving a 1 cm rim all around. (This is the secret – puff pastry rises as a result of steam, and it won't rise where there are fork pricks.)

Preheat the oven to 200 °C.

To assemble, put a thin layer of the caramelized onions on the pricked area and top with a layer of aubergine slices. Divide the Gorgonzola between the 4 tarts and drizzle a few drops of Grappa over the tarts.

Beat the egg with a fork and brush it over the unpricked area.

Bake in the oven for 15–20 minutes until the Gorgonzola has melted. Serve with a side salad of mesclun. MAKES 4 TARTS

WINE SUGGESTION: Sauvignon Blanc, a dry rosé, an unwooded Cabernet Sauvignon or a Pinot Noir

LAITUES BRAISÉE, SAUCE VIN ROUGE ACIDULÉE ET MOELLE POCHÉE

(BRAISED BUTTER LETTUCES WITH RED WINE SAUCE AND POACHED BONE MARROW)

12 small or 6 large heads
butter lettuce
1 carrot, peeled and finely chopped
1 onion, peeled and finely chopped
1 large stalk celery, finely chopped
olive oil for frying
500 ml veal or chicken stock (see
pages 148 or 149)
1 bay leaf
1 sprig thyme
salt and freshly ground black
pepper to taste
1 x recipe red wine sauce (see
page 150)
160 g raw bone marrow, off
the bone

'This is one of Frank Swainston's favourite dishes – it is delicious beyond words, melting in the mouth and slightly bitter.

'This recipe has evolved after several attempts at combining flavours, and it has proved an enormous success. Don't be intimidated by the long list of ingredients – it really is simple to make.'

Remove and discard the outer leaves of the lettuces if necessary. Plunge each head of lettuce repeatedly into boiling water to clean and soften. Refresh and drain well.

Preheat the oven to 180 °C. Sweat the chopped vegetables in a little olive oil in a baking dish or roasting pan until lightly browned. Place the lettuces horizontally on top of the vegetables. Add the stock, herbs and seasoning. Cover with foil and bake (braise) for 30–40 minutes or until soft.

In the meantime, prepare the red wine sauce.

Allow the lettuces to cool slightly. Remove the lettuce from the pan and fold each of the leaves in half toward the base. If you're using large lettuces, first cut the heads in half, through the base, then fold.

Slice the bone marrow into 5 mm-thick slices. Poach for 1 minute in boiling water. Strain and season with coarse salt and freshly ground black pepper.

To serve, warm the folded lettuce in the microwave until hot. Ladle the red wine sauce onto hot serving plates, place three lettuces on each plate and top with the bone marrow. SERVES 4

WINE SUGGESTION: Merlot, Cabernet Sauvignon, Pinotage

GRANITE
AUX ASPERGES VERTES ET À LA GRAPPA
(ASPARAGUS SORBET WITH GRAPPA)

'This is an excellent palate cleanser. In France, when you're having that supreme gastronomical experience – a seven-course meal – you have to have a break. It's called a "trou Normand" (a Norman shot); in Normandy it will be a glass of calvados – the idea is that strong alcohol will revive you. 'This is one of La Colombe's "revivers", where we've combined a vegetable with alcohol.'

150 ml water
150 g sugar
1 bunch very fresh green asparagus
50 ml Grappa

Combine the water and sugar in a saucepan to make the sugar syrup. Bring to the boil, then cool.

Peel the asparagus downwards from 2 cm below the tips. Blanch in boiling salted water for about 2 minutes, then refresh in ice-cold water to stop the cooking process. Cut off the tips of the asparagus and set aside.

Place the stalks in a blender, together with the sugar syrup and Grappa and blend until smooth.

Work this mixture in an ice-cream maker for 20 minutes. If you don't have an ice-cream maker, place the mixture in a glass dish in the freezer for 4 hours and stir with a whisk every hour or so.

Scoop the sorbet into Martini glasses and garnish with a few asparagus tips.

SERVES 4

'A main course is like a straight, smooth flight –

it's pure contentment and pleasure.'

TRANCHE DE THON GRILLÉE, EMULTION À L'ORANGE ET À LA CORIANDRE FRAÎCHE

(TUNA WITH ORANGE)

'As a teenager in Provence, I'd go fishing with friends for sea bream. We'd fill the fish with dry fennel sticks and use string to tie on slices of orange. This tuna dish, done medium-rare, reminds me of those flavours – it has the right balance of sweet and sharp.'

juice of 5 oranges, with cells strained out (or 400 ml ready-squeezed juice)

juice of 1 lemon (strain out the cells)

50 ml cream

100 g butter

salt and freshly ground black pepper to taste

4 x 220 g tuna steaks, skinned and deboned with the fat (the dark-red area) removed

olive oil for frying

1 bunch fresh coriander, chopped (save a few sprigs for garnish)

Combine juices in a pan and reduce until almost syrupy. Add the cream, reduce by half and whisk in the butter. Season at the last minute, otherwise the pepper will give a grey colour to the sauce.

Season the tuna steaks with salt and pepper on both sides. Heat a frying pan with a little olive oil and fry the steaks as you would for meat – brown on the outside, medium-rare inside. With steaks 2–3 cm thick, you'd cook them for a minute or so on each side.

To assemble, place a pinch of chopped coriander in the centre of each plate. Ladle the sauce on top so that it mixes. Slice the tuna steak into 4 thick slices and arrange on the plate.

Garnish with the remaining coriander sprigs. SERVES 4

WINE SUGGESTION: A very dry white or rosé

TRANCHE DE THON LARDÉE D'ANCHOIS, BEURRE CITRONNE AU LAURIER ET PURÉE D'AUBERGINE

(TUNA LARDED WITH ANCHOVIES, LEMON AND BAY LEAF BUTTER AND AUBERGINE PURÉE)

'Mix anchovies with any other fish (or meat,

or even vegetables) and it'll boost the flavour.

In France we eat anchovies with bread and butter.'

8 anchovy fillets

4 x 220 g tuna steaks, skinned and deboned with the fat (the dark-red area) removed

100 ml lemon juice

200 ml cream

2 bay leaves

150 g butter

1 x recipe aubergine purée (page 155)

Cut the anchovy fillets in half. With a sharp, pointed knife, make four holes in each tuna steak. Using the knife, press an anchovy half into each hole.

Reduce the lemon juice by half on a hot stove, then add the cream and the bay leaves. Reduce by half again. Whisk in the butter.

Grill the tuna steaks until medium-rare. Pour a little of the sauce onto each serving plate. Place the purée in the centre, and top with the steak. Pour over the remaining sauce. SERVES 4

WINE SUGGESTION: Uitsig Sémillon Reserve

KINGKLIP EN CROÛTE D'HERBES ET CRÈME DE CIBOULETTE

(KINGKLIP WITH A HERB AND CHEESE CRUST, WITH TOMATO CONCASSE AND A CHARDONNAY AND CHIVE CREAM)

'I love fish fingers with ketchup, but I can't possibly serve them at La Colombe. So this is a grown-up version – the crust and tomato are still there but the flavours are somewhat more sophisticated.

'I use kingklip for this dish as it is a big, firm-fleshed fish and you can cut a slice with a good height – that way you can see the texture of the fish and the layers of the dish.'

4 x 220 g thick kingklip steaks
salt and freshly ground black
pepper to taste
olive oil for frying
1 x recipe Franck's tomato
concasse (see page 150)
200 g herb crust (see page 157)
1 x recipe Franck's Chardonnay
cream sauce (see page 151)
1 bunch chives, snipped

Preheat oven to 170 °C.

Season and sear the steaks in sizzling-hot oil for about 30 seconds on each side. The fish must be raw inside, as it will still be baked.

Place in an oven pan. Use absorbent paper towel to pat the fish dry. Spread a 5-mm layer of tomato concasse over each steak.

Cut a 2-cm slice of herb crust and roll it out on your work surface. Cut it to fit the fish steak, then slide a knife underneath to lift it up. Place it on top of the fish. Repeat for each steak.

Bake the fish in the oven for 12–15 minutes.

Serve with warmed Chardonnay sauce and garnish with the chives. SERVES 4

WINE SUGGESTION: Chardonnay

PAVÉ DE SAUMON NORVÉGIEN AUX ASPERGES, SAUCE HOLLANDAISE AU PAMPLEMOUSSE

(GRILLED NORWEGIAN SALMON WITH ASPARAGUS AND GRAPEFRUIT HOLLANDAISE)

16 asparagus spears
grated rind of ½ grapefruit
2 ruby grapefruit
salt and freshly ground black
pepper to taste
4 x 150 g supremes of fresh
salmon, boned and skinned
olive oil for frying
1 x recipe Franck's hollandaise
sauce (see page 151–152)
snipped chives to garnish

Peel and cook the asparagus in boiling salted water. Refresh in ice-cold water. Grate the rind of half a grapefruit. Segment the grapefruit and keep aside on a dry cloth.

Season the salmon supremes and fry in a pan in a little hot olive oil, for 2 minutes on each side. The fish must still be medium-rare inside.

Warm the asparagus and place on a plate with the salmon. Add the grapefruit rind to the Hollandaise sauce and pour it over the fish. Garnish with the grapefruit segments and snipped chives. SERVES 4

WINE SUGGESTION: Good champagne or Uitsig Sémillon Reserve

'Salmon is delicious, succulent and versatile. I can't get enough of it: I like it raw, marinated, poached, grilled, cured, smoked or roasted. Here it's prepared in the simplest way, although it can take more robust flavours, such as red wine, mushroom jus or even meat reductions.'

EMMINCE TENDRE D'AGNEAU, TIAN DE RATATOUILLE, SAUCE BASILIC

(TENDER LAMB WITH RATATOUILLE AND BASIL SAUCE)

'I like these three flavours together

– and on their own, too.'

220 g lamb rump or loin per person, fat and sinew removed (ask your butcher to prepare it for you)

salt and freshly ground black pepper to taste

oil for frying

½ x recipe pesto alla Genovese (see page 154)

500 ml cream

1 x recipe Franck's ratatouille (see page 152–153)

Preheat the oven to 260 °C.

Season the lamb and sear in a very hot frying pan. Place on a baking tray and bake until medium to medium-rare – about 20 minutes for the rump and 12 minutes for the loin.

Leave to rest in the warming drawer while you make the basil sauce. Bring the cream to the boil, whisk in the basil pesto and reduce by a third. Blend in a blender and season to taste.

Place a serving of ratatouille on each plate and pour the basil sauce to cover the bottom of the plate. Slice the meat and arrange in a fan on the sauce. SERVES 4

WINE SUGGESTION: Merlot, Cabernet Sauvignon or Shiraz

TOURNEDOS POCHÉ À L'ANGLAISE, CRÈME DE RAIFFORT

(POACHED FILLET WITH CREAM OF HORSERADISH)

2 litres beef stock (see page 148)

4 x 220 g beef fillets (tournedos)

1 x recipe cream of horseradish
sauce (see page 152)

Bring the stock to a boil. Poach the fillets for 8 minutes for medium-rare (12 or so minutes for medium); keep the lid on the pot.

Serve with roast potatoes or Yorkshire pudding, and cream of horseradish sauce.

SERVES 4

WINE SUGGESTION: Merlot

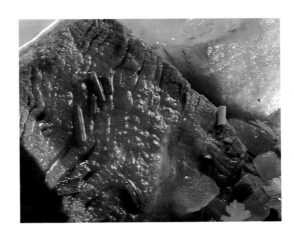

'I disagree with anyone who says English cuisine doesn't exist. I love Yorkshire pudding, and I love poached fillets – it's a great alternative to grilled or fried.

'At the restaurant we poach meat in veal stock. For home use I recommend a good stock cube – one per litre of water; it should be quite salty.'

PIGEON RÔTI, GÂTEAU DE COURGE À L'OIGNON ET SAUCE AUX BAIES DE GENIÈVRE

(ROASTED PIGEON WITH JUNIPER BERRY SAUCE AND BUTTERNUT AND ONION TIAN)

4 small pigeons, deboned

olive oil for frying

STOCK

pigeon carcasses

1 small onion, peeled and chopped

1 small carrot, peeled and chopped

1 small stalk celery, chopped

3 cloves garlic, crushed in their skin

50 ml brandy

30 ml balsamic vinegar

2 litres water

SAUCE

100 ml honey

100 ml lemon juice

400 ml pigeon stock

15 ml juniper berries

80 g butter

salt and freshly ground

black pepper to taste

BUTTERNUT AND ONION TIAN

1 small butternut, peeled,

seeded and cubed

40 g butter

5 ml sugar

pinch of ground cinnamon

1 large onion, peeled and

thinly sliced

Remove breasts and legs from pigeons and use the carcasses to make the stock. Coarsely chop the carcasses and fry in a large pot with a little very hot oil. When brown, add the vegetables and brown for a further 3 minutes. Deglaze with the brandy and balsamic vinegar and cook for 2 minutes before adding the water. Cook this stock on a gentle boil until reduced by two-thirds. Strain.

To make the sauce, place the honey in a large saucepan and boil for 3 minutes. Deglaze with lemon juice, cook for a further 3 minutes and add the stock. Reduce by half. Add the juniper berries and whisk in the butter. Season and set aside.

Place the butternut in a small saucepan with 60 ml water, cover and steam gently until the butternut is soft and the water evaporated. Add the butter, sugar and cinnamon. Mash. Fry the onions in olive oil until caramelized and soft. Season.

To assemble the tian, use a round biscuit cutter or simply stack the onion and butternut on top of each other.

To cook the pigeon, season the breasts and legs with salt and pepper.

Heat the olive oil in a frying pan and fry the legs first, skin-side down. When brown, turn over and cook gently, covered, for 5 minutes. Remove the legs and fry the breasts, also skin-side down. When brown, turn over and cook, uncovered, for 1 minute. The meat must be medium-rare. Rest the meat for 2 minutes.

Slice the breast and arrange in a fan shape. Place the butternut tian on the plate and place the legs in the centre. Pour over the sauce. SERVES 4

WINE SUGGESTION: Merlot or a Bordeaux blend

'Pigeon is my favourite game bird. Although lean, it is rich, succulent and has a complex flavour.

In the French tradition, pigeons are roasted and served with peas, braised lettuce and crispy bacon –

I prefer serving it off the bone and making concentrated flavoured jus from the carcasses.

'I like a bit of sweetness with my pigeon, like honey, dried fruits or figs and old balsamic vinegar.

Northern African spices also match pigeon beautifully.'

'This recipe is from Cape Town – from beginning to end. It's one of the few meals

where neither of my grandmothers is a source of inspiration!

'I've always loved the taste of Bobotie, as I love the spices – cloves, cinnamon, ginger, nutmeg.

But I've never had a really good Bobotie -- it's never juicy enough, and I always

have to add tons of chutney. So I chose to use those same spices to make a springbok dish.

And if anyone knows a good Bobotie recipe -- I'm looking for one ...

'If you make this dish in Europe, use pumpkin instead of butternut and venison instead of springbok.'

NOISETTES DE SPRINGBOK GRILLÉ, AU POTIRON, SAUCE AU MIEL ET ÉPICES DU CAP

(GRILLED MEDALLIONS OF SPRINGBOK WITH BUTTERNUT AND BOKAAP SPICES)

1 medium saddle of
springbok, deboned
olive oil for frying
SAUCE
100 ml honey
75 ml lemon juice
75 ml orange juice
500 ml venison stock (see
page 149)
2.5 ml each ground ginger,
cinnamon, nutmeg and cloves
2 star anise
150 g butter
salt and freshly ground black
pepper to taste
BUTTERNUT
2 small butternuts
200 ml water
30 ml sugar
50 g butter
TO GARNISH
24 skinless segments of grapefruit
or orange
1 small bunch chives, snipped
a few sprigs chervil

To make the sauce, place the honey in a medium saucepan and caramelize (boil until brown). Deglaze with the lemon and orange juice and cook for 10 minutes. Add the stock and spices and reduce the sauce by a third. Whisk in the butter, season with salt and pepper and set aside.

Peel the butternuts, cut in half and remove the pips. Cut into large cubes and place in a large pot with the water, a pinch of salt and the sugar. Cover and cook gently until the butternut is almost soft. Remove the lid and cook until the rest of the water evaporates. Stir in the butter and set aside.

Remove fat and sinew from the two loins and cut each loin into 4 pieces. Season the 8 pieces of meat on both sides with salt and freshly ground pepper. Fry in a very hot pan with a little olive oil. The meat must be crispy and cooked medium-rare.

Remove the meat from the pan and rest it for a few minutes. If you slice meat straight off the heat, the juices will run out.

Meanwhile, place a scoop of the butternut in the centre of each plate and arrange the citrus segments (3 per plate) around it.

Slice each piece of meat into three equal slices and place on the plate between the segments.

Pour warm sauce over the meat and fruit and garnish with a sprinkle of chives and a sprig of chervil.

This dish is delicious served with potato gratin. SERVES 8

WINE SUGGESTION: Cabernet Sauvignon, Shiraz or Pinotage

'I've never found tripe disgusting. My grandfather was a tripe addict so, of course, my grandmother used to make it often. I remember her buying it from the butcher and carrying it home in a big waterproof bag, then hosing it down in a metal basin. Then, from the smell of it blanching, the whole neighbourhood would know that my grandmother was cooking tripe. She would do it the traditional Provençal way, with garlic, tomatoes and black olives.

'At La Colombe, I cook tripe the same way my grandmother did, with vegetables and potatoes on the side. When you cook this dish, make enough for 8 or 12 people – in other words, double or triple this recipe. When you make a big pot, it tastes much better. And it'll keep in the refrigerator for up to two weeks, if it's well sealed.'

2 kg cleaned ox tripe

1 large carrot, peeled and cut into thick slices

1 large onion, peeled and cut into large cubes

2 large stalks celery, washed and cut into thick slices

1 head of garlic, sliced along the equator

olive oil for frying

5 fresh, very ripe tomatoes, peeled or 1 x 410 g tin of whole peeled tomatoes. (The tomatoes must be ripe. Buy them a week before and leave them outside to ripen.)

1 sprig thyme

1 strong red chilli, cut in half with the seeds still inside

1 small red pepper, seeded and diced

1 small green pepper, seeded and diced

1 small yellow pepper, seeded and diced

½ jar pitted black olives

salt and freshly ground black pepper to taste

50 g butter

Place the tripe in a large pot, cover with cold water and bring to the boil. Boil for 20 minutes. Take out the tripe and leave to cool. Reserve half the cooking water.

Cut the tripe into large strips. Remove and discard some of the fat.

In a big cast-iron pot, fry the carrot, onion, celery and garlic until lightly browned. Add the tripe strips and fry for 5 minutes.

Add the tomatoes, coarsely chopped (if using tinned tomatoes, add all the juice as well). Add the reserved cooking water, thyme and chilli. Put on the lid and place in the oven. Cook for 4 hours at 150–60 °C.

Every hour or so check that there's still moisture in the pot. Add more liquid and give it a stir if necessary. The result must have some sauce, but about half what it started out with.

In the meantime, fry the peppers in a little olive oil. Add to the tripe together with the olives during the last half hour of cooking.

Before serving, discard the chilli, season and stir in the butter.

It's possible to serve tripe immediately, but it's even better to leave it to cool in the refrigerator overnight to allow the flavours to develop. Heat and serve with boiled potatoes. SERVES 4–6

WINE SUGGESTION: Chardonnay or a good red

'Dessert is probably the dish the most looked forward to. Rich or light,

I like it simple with contrasts of smooth and crispy, hot and cold.'

ASSIETTE DE SORBETS AUX FRUITS DE SAISON

(ASSORTED SORBETS WITH FRUITS IN SEASON)

'These sorbets are a tribute to the pure

deliciousness of fruit.'

PAPAYA SORBET

1 ripe papaya, peeled, seeded and
diced

100 ml sorbet syrup (see page 153)

lemon juice as needed

KIWI SORBET

4 kiwi fruit, peeled

200 ml sorbet syrup (see page 153)

lemon juice as needed

GRANADILLA SORBET

pulp of 12 granadillas

150 ml sorbet syrup (see page 153)

lemon juice as needed

For each sorbet, blend the fruit or fruit pulp and syrup in a blender. Taste for balance of flavours and add a little lemon juice if necessary. Do not blend the granadilla pulp for more than 15 seconds or the crushed seeds will discolour the mixture. Churn in an ice-cream maker until frozen. SERVES 4

THIS RECIPE NEEDS AN ICE-CREAM MAKER

GRATIN DE FRAISES

(GRATINATED STRAWBERRIES)

4 egg yolks

15 ml ground almonds

70 g castor sugar

200 ml cream, stiffly whipped

4 punnets strawberries, halved

90 ml sugar

Cream together the yolks, almonds and castor sugar until light yellow. Fold in the whipped cream.

Place a layer of strawberries in each serving bowl (use a deep bowl, such as a soup plate). Sprinkle with sugar. Ladle two heaped tablespoons of cream mixture over the berries. Place under the grill, in the centre of the oven, until the cream is melted and brown. Serve with a scoop of orange blossom or vanilla ice cream.

SERVES 6

'In winter, make this with stewed prunes, cooked apples or pears, or citrus segments.'

SORBET AU CHOCOLAT NOIR ET FRAMBOISES À LA CRÈME

(DARK CHOCOLATE SORBET WITH CREAM AND RASPBERRIES)

100 g Belgian dark chocolate

420 ml sorbet syrup (see page 153)

100 ml water

60 g cocoa powder

cream for serving

raspberries (or orange segments)

Melt the dark chocolate on top of the stove (over simmering water) until smooth.

Heat the sorbet syrup and water together. When warm, whisk in the cocoa powder. Add the melted chocolate. Whisk until smooth.

Churn in an ice-cream maker until ready.

To serve, pour lightly whipped cream into serving bowls. Arrange the raspberries in a crown shape and scoop two balls of sorbet on top of one another.

SERVES 8

THIS RECIPE NEEDS AN ICE-CREAM MAKER

'Complicated confectionery is not my forte – I

love these simple, fruity desserts.'

CRÈME CATALANE FAÇON COLOMBE

(CATALONIAN CRÈME, LA COLOMBE STYLE)

375 ml cream

125 ml milk

5 egg yolks

1 whole egg

125 g castor sugar

grated rind of ½ lemon and

½ orange

white sugar

Preheat the oven to 130 °C.

Heat the cream and milk in a saucepan. Beat the yolks, the whole egg, sugar and rind in a bowl until light yellow. Pour the hot cream mixture over the egg mixture, stirring all the time. Return to the pan. Cook over low heat until the mixture is thick enough to coat the back of a spoon.

Divide the mixture between 8 small, shallow, ovenproof dishes and bake in a *bain marie* in the oven for about 20 minutes. Allow to cool and set. Place in the refrigerator.

Before serving, sprinkle the top with white sugar and glaze with a blowtorch. Allow the sugar to set hard. SERVES 8

'This is the ancestor of the fashionable crème brulée. Before the advent of blowtorches, the sugar used to be caramelized with a metal "brand" the same shape as the top of the dish, heated on the coals.'

FEUILLANTINE DE BAIES ROUGES ET GLACE À LA FLEUR D'ORANGER

(PUFF PASTRY FILLED WITH BERRIES AND ORANGE-BLOSSOM ICE CREAM)

400 g puff pastry (see page 157)

1 x recipe crème Anglaise (see page 153)

1 punnet blueberries

1 punnet blackberries

18 gooseberries

ICE CREAM

500 ml milk

60 ml orange blossom water (or minuscule amount of neroli oil – not even a whole drop; or grated rind of 1 orange)

6 egg yolks

150 g sugar

Make the ice cream first. Scald the milk and the flavouring in a saucepan. Cream egg yolks and sugar until light and creamy. Pour the hot milk over the egg mixture and mix well. Return to the saucepan and stir over heat until thickened. Cool. Churn in an ice-cream maker.

Roll out the pastry to just under 1-cm thick. Cut into 7-cm squares, brush with egg yolk and bake at 200 °C for about 15 minutes until risen and gold. Separate the lids from the base.

Pour a little crème Anglaise onto the bottom of the serving plate. Place the pastry base in the centre. Add a large scoop of ice cream and sprinkle with the berries. Top with the lid. SERVES 6

'Orange blossom water is a common ingredient in Provençal confectionery. You may find it in the local pharmacy and fine linen stores. I use neroli oil, from the flower of the orange; one drop is enough for three litres of ice cream. 'If you can't find anything similar, plain old vanilla is still delicious.'

THIS RECIPE NEEDS AN ICE-CREAM MAKER

TERRINE DE CHOCOLAT NOIR, SAUCE FUDGE
(DARK CHOCOLATE TERRINE WITH FUDGE SAUCE)

'During the restaurant's first few months, I had no chocolate dessert on the menu –
a cause of much sorrow among our guests.

'So I created this dish, and decided that if I was going to make a chocolate dessert, I may
as well do something completely decadent.

'This is now the most popular dessert on the menu – no matter how full anyone may be!'

1 x recipe Franck's fudge sauce
(see page 153)
BISCUIT
5 eggs, separated
50 g castor sugar
25 g ground almonds
25 g ground hazelnuts
25 g icing sugar
grated rind of 1 orange
MOUSSE
4 egg yolks
140 g castor sugar
160 g butter, softened
75 g cocoa powder
75 g dark chocolate, melted (I use
Belgian chocolate.)
275 ml cream
25 g icing sugar

Preheat the oven to 200 °C. Grease a baking tray and line it with greaseproof paper. Grease and flour the paper.

To make the biscuit, cream the egg yolks and castor sugar until light and creamy. Add nuts and mix well. Beat egg whites until stiff. Add the icing sugar and beat for another minute. Fold the stiff egg whites into the yolk mixture. Add the orange rind. Spread the mixture evenly in the baking tray and bake for 10–15 minutes or until lightly golden and springy when pressed. While hot, cut the biscuit into 5 rectangles, each one slightly smaller than the base of the loaf tin. Set aside.

To make the mousse, cream the egg yolks and castor sugar until light and creamy. Add the butter and beat well. Add the cocoa alternatively with chocolate and mix well. Whip the cream until stiff. Beat in the icing sugar. Fold the cream into the chocolate mixture.

To assemble, oil the loaf tin, then line it with plastic wrap. Place one biscuit into the tin and spread with a quarter of the mousse. Repeat with the next biscuit layer and mousse, finishing with biscuit. Refrigerate for at least 5 hours.

Turn out of the mould and use a thin, long, hot knife to slice the terrine. Serve with the fudge sauce. MAKES 1 LOAF, SERVES 14

SPAANSCHEMAT RIVER CAFÉ

'Beautifully presented,

enticingly aromatic and

deliciously tasty – good food

should appeal to the senses.'

Judy Badenhorst and Graham Isaacson

'Your grandmother was right – breakfast really is the most

important meal of the day. And what better meal to take advantage

of the succulent fresh and dried fruits of the Cape.'

SPICED FRUIT COMPOTE

'This makes an excellent light morning meal,

especially if you want to go out for breakfast

or to serve a cooked dish but don't feel like eggs yet again.'

6 rooibos tea bags
1 litre hot water
250 ml honey
2 large cinnamon sticks
1 lemon, sliced
500 g dried mixed fruit (prunes, apricots, peaches, etc)
200 g thick plain yoghurt
30 ml honey for drizzling
ground cinnamon
toasted almonds

Steep the tea bags in the hot water. Add the honey and dissolve. Add the cinnamon and lemon.

Pour over the dried fruit and bring to a gentle simmer on the stove for 45 minutes. Add more water towards the end, if necessary.

Allow to stand for at least 12 hours.

Serve with the yoghurt and honey and top with cinnamon and nuts. SERVES 16

Yoghurt terrine
with fresh fruit and granola

'A really good alternative to yoghurt for a fresh and healthy start to the morning.

It's also wonderful as a dessert with soft summer fruits.'

500 ml cream

15 g gelatine powder

75 g castor sugar

500 ml Greek yoghurt

10 ml vanilla extract

granola

STRAWBERRY COULIS

500 g strawberries

150 g castor sugar

fresh fruit (granadillas, raspberries,

blackberries, loganberries,

mangoes, kiwi fruit)

Place 45 ml of the cream with the gelatine in a cup and soak for 10 minutes.

Place the rest of the cream with the castor sugar in a pan and heat. Add the gelatine to the warm cream and whisk it. Remove from the heat.

In a bowl, mix together the yoghurt and vanilla, then add the cream mixture. Pour the mixture into a 18 cm x 8 cm loaf tin that is lined with plastic wrap. Once it's cool, cover and refrigerate overnight or for 4–6 hours until set.

Make the coulis by blending all the ingredients in a blender until smooth.

To serve, turn out the terrine, remove plastic wrap and slice into 2 cm-thick slices. Arrange each slice on a plate and spoon over a little of the coulis. Decorate with fresh fruit and serve with granola. MAKES 1 LOAF TIN

SWEETCORN AND RICOTTA BLINIS
WITH CRISPY BACON AND PRICKLY PEAR SYRUP

'We don't garnish our blinis,
as the incredible cerise colour of the syrup
against a white plate is sensational enough as it is.'

250 ml corn kernels off the cob
100 g ricotta
2 large eggs
125 ml cake flour
15 ml chopped fresh parsley
15 ml snipped chives
5 ml ground coriander
salt and freshly ground black
pepper to taste
butter for frying
streaky bacon, 4 rashers per
person
prickly pear syrup (if you can't find
any, use maple syrup) for serving

Combine all the ingredients, except the butter, bacon and syrup, in a bowl and allow to stand for at least 30 minutes.

Melt butter in a medium griddle pan, place heaped tablespoonfuls of the mixture into the pan and fry until golden-brown on each side.

Fry the bacon until crisp.

Place one blini on a heated plate, put a few rashers on top and top with another blini. Pour over a generous helping of prickly pear syrup. SERVES 10

EGGS BENEDICT ON A POTATO ROSTI

'Sometimes we sit and eavesdrop on breakfast parties:

"The most delicious way to eat eggs";"Absolutely divine";

"I'd travel across Cape Town for this" ... '

2 large potatoes, grated

30 ml chopped fresh parsley

1 egg

30 ml cake flour

salt and freshly ground black
pepper to taste

oil for frying

streaky bacon, 4 rashers per
person (for vegetarians we fry a
portion of mushrooms or
tomatoes instead)

2 eggs per person

HOLLANDAISE SAUCE

1 egg

1 egg yolk

freshly ground black pepper
to taste

5 ml lemon juice

250 g butter

Add all the ingredients, except the bacon and eggs to the grated potato.

Spoon a healthy amount of the mixture onto a hot griddle, and flatten to form a round fritter. Fry until golden on both sides.

Fry the bacon until crisp. Poach the eggs.

To make the sauce, combine the egg, egg yolk, pepper and lemon juice in a food processor. Allow the mixture to combine well. Bring the butter to the boil. With the motor running, slowly pour in the butter (it must be bubbling). Stop the processor immediately. The mixture should be medium-thick and creamy.

To serve, place a rosti on a warm plate. Cover with bacon and top with the eggs. Spoon over a generous portion of the hollandaise sauce. MAKES 8–10 ROSTI

'Flavours and textures that deliver the promise made

by the shapes and colours of the dish ... plus a surprise or two.

That's the perfect lunch.'

GRILLED KINGKLIP
WITH CHILLI HERB TOPPING

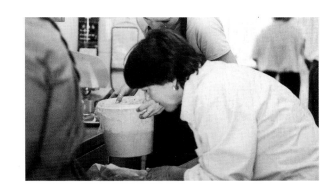

'This is one of our favourite alfresco-style dishes,

as it isn't too heavy, yet is a "real" meal.'

2 thick slices white bread

60 ml chopped fresh parsley

1–3 green chillies

15 ml butter, melted

salt and freshly ground black

pepper to taste

30 ml butter

4 x 180 g kingklip fillets

SAUCE

60 ml butter

3 tomatoes, peeled, seeded

and cubed

30–45 ml lemon juice

25 ml chopped fresh coriander

salt and freshly ground black

pepper to taste

fresh coriander to garnish

Place the bread in a food processor and process to crumbs. Add the parsley and chillies and process until fine – the bread must not form a paste. Turn out into a bowl and add the melted butter and seasoning. Set aside.

Preheat the oven to 260 °C.

Heat the butter in a frying pan until foaming. Fry the fillets for about 1 minute each side. Remove from the pan, cool slightly and press the herb chilli mixture onto each fillet – the crust should be quite thick.

Place the prepared fish onto a foil-covered baking tray and bake for 8 minutes.

To make the sauce, melt the butter in a pan. Add the tomato and sauté gently for 2 minutes. Add the lemon juice and coriander and swirl around in the pan.

Check for seasoning.

To serve, place a large tablespoon of the sauce on a plate and place fish on top. Decorate with fresh coriander. SERVES 4

WINE SUGGESTION: Sauvignon Blanc

WARM SALAD
OF CHICKPEAS, CHILLI, FETA AND GARLIC

'This salad is very popular – yet I'd guess that few people would serve chickpeas at home. But don't be intimidated by pulses – they're coming back into food fashion, and with a little care are really easy to prepare. And they go well with almost any flavour and dressing.'

300 g dried chickpeas or 2 x 410 g
tins, drained
3 red chillies, seeded and
finely sliced
12 cloves garlic, peeled and
roughly chopped
3 red onions, peeled and
finely sliced
200 ml olive oil
150 ml cider vinegar
250 ml fresh coriander leaves
250 ml fresh flat-leaf parsley leaves
250 ml roughly crumbled feta
250 ml sliced spring onions
250 ml fresh mint leaves
125 ml extra-virgin olive oil
salt and freshly ground black
pepper to taste

If you're using dried chickpeas, soak them overnight in plenty of cold water. Drain and rinse, then decant into a deep pot. Add enough cold water to submerge them by at least 5 cm and bring to the boil before turning down to a rapid simmer. Skim off any scrum that forms during cooking. Keep topping up with boiling water so the peas don't dry out. Depending on the size of the chickpea, they'll need to cook for 1–2 hours. When cooked, drain well and rinse under hot water.

Fry the chilli, garlic and onions in the olive oil over a high heat for 5 minutes – stir to prevent sticking. Add the vinegar and boil until it has evaporated.

Mix the chickpeas and onion mix together in a large bowl. Add the remaining ingredients and mix very well.

Leave to rest for 15 minutes, then stir and check for seasoning. SERVES 6

WINE SUGGESTION: Sémillon

SPICED FILLET OF BEEF SALAD WITH ROCKET AND NOODLES

300 ml soy sauce

1 red chilli

9 cloves garlic

handful fresh coriander leaves

100 ml olive oil

1 beef fillet (1.3 kg), trimmed

DRESSING

250 ml soy sauce

5 cm fresh ginger, peeled

and sliced

1 red chilli

45 ml lemon juice

15 ml Thai fish sauce

15 ml brown sugar

4 cloves garlic

handful fresh coriander

NOODLE SALAD

300 g spaghetti or fresh Chinese

noodles (or any egg noodles)

rocket leaves

mung bean sprouts

fresh coriander

Place the soy sauce, chilli, garlic, coriander and olive oil in a blender and blend until smooth. Pour over the fillet and leave overnight or for at least 4 hours, turning several times. Drain well. Roast at 220 °C for 20 minutes. Allow to cool.

Blend together all the dressing ingredients.

Cook the noodles or pasta according to packet instructions and drain well.

Arrange the rocket leaves on a large platter or individual plates. Put a small pile of noodles in the centre and arrange the thinly sliced rare fillet around them. Drizzle with the dressing and top with bean sprouts and fresh coriander. SERVES 6

WINE SUGGESTION: Weisser Riesling or Shiraz

MEDITERRANEAN LAYERED CRÊPE CAKE

'This is an old favourite, which we adapted from *The Greens Cookbook* by Deborah Madison and Edward Espe Brown. It is a wonderful standby as it can be assembled the day before and heated when required. The fillings can also be varied according to your taste. This variation has wonderful Mediterranean flavours and is particularly colourful. We serve it with a small green salad.'

9 large crêpes (see page 158)
500 g courgettes, coarsely grated
salt
10 ml chopped fresh mixed herbs
45 ml olive oil
freshly ground black
pepper to taste
250 ml pitted black olives
2 cloves garlic
500 ml tomato and basil sauce
(page 149)
60 ml freshly grated Parmesan
240 g Cheddar, grated

Make the crêpes according to the recipe. Sprinkle courgettes with a little salt and set aside for 30 minutes to draw out the juice, then squeeze out the liquid with your hands. Cook the courgettes and herbs in 15 ml olive oil, stirring until most of the liquid has evaporated. Season with salt and pepper. Put olives, garlic and remaining olive oil in a food processor and chop finely to form an olive paste.

To assemble, butter a baking dish. Lay down one crêpe and brush with 15 ml tomato and basil sauce. Sprinkle with 15 ml Parmesan and cover with a third of the courgette mixture. Add second crêpe, cover with 15 ml tomato sauce and a third of the olive paste. Add a third crêpe, brush with tomato sauce and cover with half the Cheddar. Repeat the first three layers. Next, add a crêpe, brush with tomato sauce, followed by courgette mixture. Add another crêpe and top with tomato sauce and remaining olive paste. Cover with the remaining crêpe, brush with tomato sauce and sprinkle with remaining Parmesan. Cover loosely with foil and bake for 15 minutes at 200 °C. Remove foil and bake for a further 10 minutes or microwave on high for 6 minutes. Serve a wedge on a plate with a fresh tomato coulis, roasted peppers, olives or garnish of your choice. SERVES 6

WINE SUGGESTION: Pinot Noir

SMOKED SALMON, CELERIAC AND APPLE SALAD IN CUMIN CREAM

1 celeriac bulb, raw
2 sour apples
30 ml lemon juice
60 g smoked salmon or
salmon trout per person
soft-leafed lettuce
lemon wedges
15 ml snipped chives
DRESSING
100 ml cream
50 ml olive oil
salt and freshly ground black
pepper to taste
pinch of sugar
30 ml lemon juice
20 ml freshly ground cumin

'The secret is the cumin, freshly ground in a pestle and mortar.
I tasted celeriac for the first time upstairs at Fortnum and Mason's,
years ago. I went downstairs and bought a whole bulb,
and packed it in my bags to bring back home.
Now I find them at Cape Town's V&A Waterfront.'

Combine all the dressing ingredients and allow to stand, refrigerated, for at least 1 hour. It will slowly thicken.

Peel the outer skin off the celeriac. Slice the flesh into discs, then into thin julienne strips. Do the same with the apples. Leave covered, with a little lemon juice squeezed over, in the refrigerator.

Cut the salmon into wide strips and combine with the celeriac and apple.

To serve, place a heap of the salmon mixture in the centre of a plate. Surround with lettuce and a wedge of lemon.

Spoon over the cumin dressing and garnish with chives. SERVES 4

WINE SUGGESTION: Sauvignon Blanc

GREEN FIG PRESERVE

100 green figs
5 litres water
30 ml salt
6 litres water
4 kg sugar
5 pieces dried root ginger
juice of 3 lemons

Cut a cross on the base of each fig. Mix water and salt and soak figs in brine solution overnight. Drain well. Put figs in water to cover, bring to the boil and cook until tender but not soft. Drain figs and gently press out the water, without breaking the figs.

Bring the 6 litres of water and the sugar to the boil, stirring to dissolve the sugar. Drop in the figs and ginger and boil until the figs are transparent and syrup has thickened. Add lemon juice and boil for a further 5 minutes. Skim off the scum. Fill sterilized bottes with the hot figs and cover with syrup. Replace vacuum-sealed lids. MAKES 10 x 450 ML JARS.

WINE SUGGESTION: Vin de Constance

'This is a real Cape tradition.

Serve the green fig preserve with gorgonzola

and sweet potato bread as a perfect ending to a meal.

The sweetness of the figs perfectly

complements the cheese.'

SWEET POTATO BREAD

500 g sweet potatoes, peeled
and diced
400 ml milk
800 g bread or cake flour
5 ml salt
45 ml instant dry yeast
milk
coarse salt
5 ml cumin seeds (optional)

Cook sweet potato in the milk until soft. Remove potato with a slotted spoon, then boil the milk until it has reduced by half. Put both the potato and the milk in a bowl and allow to cool.

Place flour, salt and yeast in a bowl and mix well. Add sweet potato and milk and knead well for 5 minutes (by hand or in a food mixer). The dough should be moist but not sticky. Leave in a warm place until doubled in size.

Punch down the dough and form into two long oval shapes. Place on floured baking trays until well risen.

Preheat the oven to 180 °C. Brush dough with milk and sprinkle with coarse salt (and seeds, if you wish). Bake for 20–30 minutes or until golden brown. MAKES 2 x 750 G LOAVES

'Sweet potato is one of the café's staple foods;

baked, roasted, made into soups,

served in so many ways.

This bread is slightly chewy with a nice crust, and is

excellent toasted the next day.'

'We love desserts that are light, luscious and lovely.

And voluptuous cakes that taste as good as they look ... we can't

resist them, and neither can our guests at the River Café.'

CINNAMON MERINGUE PAVLOVA
WITH TIRAMISU FILLING

'This is a multi-purpose recipe.
The tiramisu can be served separately, and any filling
of your choice, such as chocolate mousse, or fresh
cream and fruit, can be used for the pavlova.'

6 extra large egg whites
330 g castor sugar
5 ml ground cinnamon
TIRAMISU FILLING
6 egg yolks
80 g castor sugar
100 ml sherry
30 ml preferred liqueur
375 ml cream
grated rind of 1 lemon
15 boudoir biscuits
125 ml strong cold black coffee

To make the meringue, whisk egg whites until stiff. Slowly add the castor sugar and beat thoroughly until sugar is dissolved. Sift cinnamon onto meringue mixture and fold in gently. Spoon the mixture into a circle on a prepared baking tray. Use a spatula to mound up the sides and to make a slight depression on top. Bake for 1 hour at 140 °C.

For the filling, beat the egg yolks and castor sugar and add the sherry and liqueur. Beat the cream and fold it gently into the yolk mixture together with the lemon rind.

Dip biscuits in coffee and arrange in a dish. Spread cream mixture on top. Continue alternating biscuits and cream mixture until mixture is finished, ending with a layer of cream mixture. Refrigerate for at least 45 minutes before serving. Spoon the filling into the cinnamon meringue and decorate as desired.
SERVES 8–10

BASICS

'These basics are the foundations of beautiful food, the food we love to prepare and serve. Without them the subtle flavours, the flavours that really make the difference, will simply not be there. So try them, even if they look tiring!

'The secret is to enjoy every part of the cooking – for me, making bread is as enjoyable as assembling a dish and serving it (and watching the reactions of my guests). If you're going to embark on a new dish for friends, one that involves making pastry or pasta or reducing sauces, don't get in a panic – simply ask your friends to arrive early and help you. Enjoy it from beginning to end.'

STOCKS

'For stocks, it's always best to use crisp, fresh vegetables, but it's perfectly OK to use slightly aged ingredients if you have to. Rather make a stock with soft vegetables than not make a stock at all.'

FISH STOCK

In the Northern Hemisphere, the best bones to use are Dover sole or turbot. In the Southern Hemisphere, we use monkfish or sole. Even Cape salmon and kob make great stock. Use the stock for poaching fish and shellfish, or in fish sauces.'

1.8–2 kg fish bones
½ large onion, finely sliced
1 large stalk celery, finely sliced
1 large leek, white part only, finely sliced
1 carrot, scraped and finely sliced
½ head garlic, cloves peeled
15 ml olive oil
200 ml white wine
1 lemon, sliced
2 litres cold water

Wash the fish bones very thoroughly and chop. Cook the vegetables and garlic in the oil for a few minutes to soften, but without allowing them to colour. Add the bones, wine and lemon and cook for 5 minutes.

Add the water and bring to the boil. Skim, then simmer for 20 minutes.

Pass through a fine sieve and cool. Store in the refrigerator for 1 day only or freeze (for no longer than a month)

MAKES ABOUT 2 LITRES

VEAL/BEEF STOCK

3 kg veal or beef knuckle bones
3 carrots, cut in quarters
1 onion, peeled and quartered
3 stalks celery, cut in quarters
1 small head garlic, cut in half horizontally (as if around the equator)
cooking oil
60 ml tomato purée
1 bouquet garni (bay leaf, thyme, parsley stalk – parsley leaves will make the stock turn dark)
10 litres cold water

Roast the knuckle bones in the oven until golden brown.

In the meantime, cook the vegetables in a large pot in a little oil until golden brown.

Add the tomato purée and the bouquet garni and brown a little more. Be careful not to burn. Take off the heat.

When the bones are roasted, place in the pot along with the vegetables, cover with the water, bring to the boil and skim. Allow to simmer for 8–10 hours, topping up with water when necessary to keep the bones covered.

Pass through a fine sieve and into a tall pan. Boil to reduce by half, then cool.

This stock can be stored in the refrigerator for up to a week or in the freezer for up to 3 months.

MAKES 3 LITRES

VEGETABLE STOCK

Follow the instructions for Chicken Stock (opposite) but leave out the chicken and add a few extra leeks and some potatoes.

VENISON STOCK

1.5 kg springbok bones

1 large carrot, peeled and
    coarsely chopped

1 large onion, peeled and
    coarsely chopped

1 large stalk celery, coarsely
    chopped

1 small head garlic, cut in half
    horizontally

60 ml olive oil

5 litres water

200 ml red wine

30 ml tomato purée

Roast the bones in a hot
oven until golden brown.

   In a very large pot, fry the
vegetables in oil until brown.
Add the bones and cover
with the water, wine and
tomato purée. Bring to the
boil, reduce the heat and
simmer gently for 6–8 hours,
adding a little more water as
it reduces. Strain through a
fine sieve, return to the heat
and reduce by two-thirds.

   Store in the refrigerator
and skim any fat from the
surface when cold.

MAKES ABOUT 1.5 LITRES

CHICKEN STOCK

*'Chicken stock is used
because it has no colour,
but is particularly
flavourful – if you brown
the chicken bones first,
you'll have a brown stock.'*

3 kg chicken carcasses

3 carrots, cut in four

2 leeks, cleaned and roughly
    chopped – use the white
    parts and some of the green

1 onion, peeled and cut in
    quarters

3 stalks celery, cut in
    quarters

1 small head garlic, cut in half
    horizontally

1 bouquet garni

10 litres cold water

Put everything in a pot, pour
over the water and bring to
the boil. Let it simmer for
about 2 hours – it will reduce
at the same time.

   Pass through a fine sieve.
Cool. Store in the refrigerator
for up to a week or in the
freezer for up to 3 months.

MAKES ABOUT 8 LITRES

SAUCES

'The secret of good sauces and stocks is in the
reducing. We don't use that many ingredients,
but we concentrate the flavours. And reducing is
the only way to do this.

'The wider the pan and the higher the heat, the
more quickly the sauce will reduce.
Don't put the lid on, as the liquid will condense
and fall back into the pot.'

FRANK'S SALSA POMMAROLA (TOMATO AND BASIL SAUCE)

*'Certain combinations are
made in heaven, like
tomato and basil. I love
to thickly slice red, ripe
tomatoes, sprinkle them
with coarse salt, good
olive oil and chopped basil
and leave them for an
hour. Then I eat them
with bread and butter.
Delicious'*

1 large onion, finely sliced

1 stalk celery, finely chopped

1 large carrot, finely grated

2 cloves garlic, finely chopped

olive oil for frying

15 ml tomato paste

410 g tin chopped Italian
    tomatoes

1 small bunch fresh basil, finely
    chopped

salt and freshly ground black
    pepper to taste

Fry all the vegetables in the
oil with the tomato paste,
stirring all the time. When
the oil comes to the top,
slowly add the tomatoes and
the basil. Season to taste and
cook slowly for 1 hour.

MAKES ABOUT 500 ml

FRANCK'S RED WINE SAUCE

'At La Colombe we serve this with braised lettuce. It's just as good with fish (use fish stock, page 148) or meat (use meat stock, page 148).'

2 shallots, peeled and finely chopped
butter for frying
650 ml good red table wine
80 ml red port
250 ml beef, fish or chicken stock
50 ml cream
100 g butter
salt and pepper to taste

Sweat the shallots in butter until transparent. Add the wine and port. Reduce by two-thirds. Add the stock and reduce by half. Add the cream and simmer for 5 minutes, then whisk in the 100 g butter. Season to taste. Serve hot.
MAKES ABOUT 300 ML

FRANCK'S SWEET CHILLI SAUCE

'I'm addicted to chilli – I love them red, I love them green; fresh or dried; in sauces or on their own; bread and butter and chilli; scrambled eggs and chilli ... Once your mouth is on fire, your tastebuds discover things they've never known before.

'In France we have that piment d'Esplette – *the most amazing chilli – a chilli that's not so strong but has lots of flavour. So you can add a load of chilli flavour without the heat.*

'Serve this sauce with fish, prawns, chicken, salads ...'

100 ml water
100 g castor sugar
60 ml white wine vinegar
5 ml corn starch, diluted with a little water
5 ml finely chopped red chilli (with the seeds)
2.5 ml finely chopped garlic

In a saucepan, combine the water, sugar and vinegar. Bring to the boil, then whisk in the corn starch. Remove from heat and add the chilli and garlic. Whisk, leave to cool, then refrigerate. The sauce will last for about 2 weeks if stored in a tightly sealed jar.
MAKES ABOUT 300 ML

FRANCK'S TOMATO CONCASSE

'This is a recipe from my grandmother. She used to make it at the peak of summer, when her garden was filled with ripe tomatoes, bursting with flavour. We would eat tomatoes every day.

'When I make it at home, I double the amount of oil – the oil turns bright red – and drizzle it on bread.

'Because this sauce is so reduced, it will keep longer than a fresh sauce. It also freezes well, and is great on fish, meat, baked potatoes and pasta.'

100 ml olive oil
½ small onion, finely chopped
1 clove garlic, peeled and finely chopped
6–8 large, ripe plum tomatoes, skinned, seeded and coarsely chopped (If you use tinned tomatoes, you'll need to strain out the juice – make a Bloody Mary to drink while you're cooking!)
1 sprig thyme
½ small bay leaf
salt and freshly ground black pepper to taste

Heat the olive oil in a pan. Sweat the onion and garlic until transparent. Add the chopped tomato, thyme and bay leaf and cook gently until you're left with a thick, dry tomato paste rich in flavour. Season with salt and pepper. Take out the whole herbs and leave the sauce chunky.
MAKES ABOUT 150 ML

FRANCK'S CHARDONNAY CREAM SAUCE FOR FISH AND SEAFOOD

'This is an old classic recipe – no grandmothers involved this time!'

2 shallots, peeled and chopped
25 g butter
400 ml Chardonnay
½ small bay leaf
400 ml fish stock
   (see page 148)
400 ml cream
salt and freshly ground black
   pepper to taste

Sweat the shallots in the butter until transparent. Add the wine and bay leaf and reduce by a third. Add the fish stock and reduce by a third. Add the cream and reduce by a third again. Blend the sauce to crush the shallots. Add salt and pepper and serve hot.
MAKES ABOUT 400 ML

FRANK'S SPICY ORIENTAL SAUCE

'To me, Indian and Chinese are two of the greatest cuisines of the world – and this sauce has the two coming together perfectly.

'At Uitsig we serve it with line fish.'

450 ml honey
400 ml white wine vinegar
1 bunch fresh coriander
5 ml English mustard powder
   (Coleman's)
150 ml sesame oil
3 ml each ground allspice,
   coriander, cumin, Chinese
   five-spice mix, cloves,
   caraway seeds, fennel
   seeds, black pepper, star
   anise, turmeric, ginger
15 ml Madras curry powder
1.2 litres meat stock, simmered
   to reduce to
   500 ml (it will have a jelly-like
   consistency [demi-glace])
fresh red chilli to taste
15 ml chopped shallots or
   spring onions

In a saucepan, reduce the honey and vinegar to a caramel. Add the fresh coriander, mustard powder, sesame oil and all the other spices. Simmer for 3 minutes, remove from heat and cool.

In a separate pan, heat the demi-glace to a boil, then pour over the cooled spice mixture. Leave to cool, then pass through a fine sieve.

Before serving, fry the chilli and shallots and add to the sauce.
MAKES ABOUT 400 ML

FRANCK'S LA SAUCE PALETTA

4 ripe, medium tomatoes,
   peeled
15 fresh basil leaves
100 ml olive oil
30 ml red wine vinegar
salt and freshly ground black
   pepper to taste

Combine all the ingredients in a blender and blend until smooth.
MAKES ABOUT 200 ML

CRÈME DE RAIFFORT (CREAM OF HORSERADISH SAUCE)

'Fresh horseradish is delicious sliced very thinly and eaten with bread, butter and salt.'

2 shallots or 1 small onion,
   peeled and finely chopped
olive oil for frying
50 ml white wine
15 ml white wine vinegar
200 ml cream
45 ml creamed horseradish
salt and white pepper to taste

Fry the shallots or onion in a little oil until transparent. Deglaze with the wine and vinegar. Bring to a boil and add the cream. Return to a gentle boil and cook for 3 minutes. Add the creamed horseradish (this will thicken your sauce). Add salt and pepper to taste.
MAKES ABOUT 250 ML

FRANCK'S HOLLANDAISE SAUCE

'This is the mother of all sauces, the queen of butters. It's one of the first sauces I learned to make, and when you get it right, it's fantastic. It's not an easy sauce to get right, so it's very rewarding – extraordinarily fluffy and delicious.

'Of course, it's also pure fat! Nevertheless, when you have it, have lots of it. Serve it on steamed vegetables to appease your guilt.'

300 g butter

2 egg yolks

juice of 1 lemon

40 ml water

salt and cayenne pepper to taste

First make your clarified butter; butter is fat, salt and buttermilk, so when you clarify it, you get rid of the buttermilk and the salt. To do this, put the butter in a *bain marie* and warm the water until the butter melts. Don't stir, or it will emulsify. You'll have foam on the top, clarified butter in the middle and buttermilk at the bottom. Scoop out the clarified butter and discard the rest.

Place the egg yolks in a bowl with half the lemon juice. Whisk together, then gradually whisk in the water until you have a nice sabayon (at the fluffy, ribbon stage). The liquid must be added slowly.

After about 10 minutes of whipping (if the prospect exhausts you, use an electric whisk), put the bowl over a *bain marie* and gradually add the warm, clarified butter. Whip until you have a good emulsion. The sauce should be thick and fluffy.

Add the rest of the lemon juice, salt and cayenne pepper. SERVES 4

FRANCK'S RATATOUILLE

'If I had to take one dish to the moon, this would be it – I'll never get tired of it.

'It's a dish that represents the essence of southern French cuisine – colourful, flavoursome, generous, textured, rich. The ultimate is when it's served ice cold on a toasted baguette, with olive oil and freshly chopped basil.

'My grandmother used to make ratatouille. She would cut the vegetables into large, egg-sized chunks and roast them all in the oven with olive oil, then combine them in a pot. It would cook on the stove for hours, it seemed to be as a child, because of the size of the chunks. I'd be starving by the time it was ready.

'She used to put tomatoes in ratatouille, so so do I – whatever any purists might say!

'You can't make this dish for four – it has to made in a large pot, in large quantities. The flavour is better, somehow.'

5 very ripe plum tomatoes

salt and freshly ground black pepper to taste

olive oil

2 onions, peeled and cubed

2 medium red peppers, seeded and cut into squares

1 medium yellow pepper, seeded and cut into squares

1 medium green pepper, seeded and cut into squares

5 courgettes, ends removed and cut into thick slices (or 2 courgettes and 3 patty pans)

2 large aubergines, cubed

10 small cloves garlic

20 ml chopped garlic

lots of basil – about 20 leaves, chopped. (Keep the stalks and tie them in a bundle with a bit of string.)

Halve the tomatoes and bake at 180 °C for 15 minutes, with salt, pepper and a little

DESSERT SAUCES AND SYRUPS

'Home-made custard, home-made fudge sauce and home-made
ice cream – there's little to beat them.'

olive oil. Leave to cool, then cut in half again. Set aside.

Fry all the vegetables, except the garlic, individually in olive oil in a large frying pan until the edges begin to brown. Lightly season every batch in the pan.

Strain in a colander to drain excess oil.

In a large cast-iron pot, fry the garlic cloves in olive oil, until they begin to brown. Add the chopped garlic and fry for a few seconds. Add the rest of the cooked vegetables. Stir gently.

Add the bundle of basil stalks. Cover with a lid and simmer very gently over low heat for about 40 minutes. Add the tomatoes and cook for another 20 minutes.

Season with salt and pepper. Just before serving, add the chopped basil and stir lightly.

SERVES 8, AS AN
ACCOMPANIMENT TO
EGGS, LAMB, FISH

FRANCK'S FUDGE SAUCE

400 g sugar

100 ml water

1 litre cream

Place the sugar and water in a heavy-bottomed saucepan. Heat to dissolve the sugar. Once dissolved, bring to the boil and simmer until caramelized and brown. Deglaze with cream and stir, while simmering, until smooth. Leave to cool.

MAKES ABOUT 1.5 LITRES
(SERVES 14)

FRANK'S ORANGE CRÈME ANGLAISE

'Every Sunday afternoon of my English childhood, my mother would serve cakes and tarts in the "smart" lounge of our home – after we'd already eaten a full roast for lunch. She'd have spent hours in the kitchen, and hot custard was always on the menu – Birds' custard powder, of course. So the good old days weren't always the way we think they should have been!'

8 egg yolks

120 g castor sugar

500 ml cream

500 ml milk

10 ml vanilla essence or
  1 vanilla pod

1 large piece orange rind

1 tot Van der Hum – optional

Beat the egg yolks and mix in the sugar.

In a saucepan, bring the cream and milk to the boil with the vanilla pod and orange rind. Remove from heat and whisk in the egg mixture (if you're using vanilla essence, add it now). Remove the vanilla pod and orange rind. Add the liqueur and blend in a blender.

MAKES ABOUT 1 LITRE

SORBET SYRUP

600 ml water

400 g castor sugar

Combine in a pot. Bring to the boil, then set aside to cool.

MAKES ABOUT 1 LITRE

DRESSINGS AND DIPS

'There's no excuse not to make a dressing –

they're so easy and are much, much better than the bought versions.'

FRANK'S HOME-MADE MAYONNAISE

'I like mayonnaise to be made with olive oil only, but many people find the taste too strong. If you'd prefer, use half olive oil, half sunflower.

This recipe keeps for a week or even longer, so it's worth preparing extra. If you have a blender, it's the easiest thing to make.'

3 eggs
3 ml Coleman's mustard
   powder
salt and ground white pepper
   to taste
500 ml olive oil
fresh lemon juice or good white
   wine vinegar to taste

Using a blender, whisk together the eggs and mustard powder. Season.

With the motor running, pour the olive oil slowly into the egg mixture until it emulsifies. Add the lemon juice or vinegar to taste.

If the mixture breaks down, add a little warm water and stir. If it becomes too runny, add another egg yolk. MAKES 500 ML

PESTO ALLA GENOVESE

'This classic recipe is made with fresh summer basil and garlic. It's enough for about 700 g of pasta.'

4 large cloves garlic
coarse salt
30 ml pine nuts, toasted
8 small bunches fresh basil
30 ml or more olive oil
60 ml grated Parmesan

Use a blender, which is quick and effective, and blend the garlic, salt, pine nuts and basil with a little of the olive oil. Add more olive oil and the Parmesan. Blend further – don't make it too smooth; you should still be able to see the pine nuts. SERVES 6

FRANK'S VINAIGRETTE

'The addition of soy sauce in this recipe gives it a more complex taste.'

75 ml white or red wine vinegar
15 ml Dijon mustard
salt and pepper to taste
120 ml sunflower oil
200 ml olive oil
dried Provençal herbs –
   rosemary, thyme, basil
dash of Kikkoman's
   soy sauce

Place vinegar and mustard in a bowl and add the salt and pepper. Stir with a whisk to dissolve. Add the oils, herbs and soy sauce and stir to an emulsion.
MAKES ABOUT 400 ML

FRANCK'S VINAIGRETTE

'This is the classic French vinaigrette. South Africans seem to buy their vinaigrette in bottles – in France, everyone can whip this up in a coffee cup without thinking twice. Try it – it is so easy and the variations are endless: sugar, apple cider vinegar, a pinch of paprika, olive oil and lemon juice ... What's important is the balance of sourness and acidity.'

75 ml white or red wine vinegar

15 ml Dijon mustard

salt and freshly ground black
 pepper to taste

120 ml sunflower oil (I prefer
 sunflower oil.)

200 ml olive oil

Place vinegar and mustard in a bowl and add the salt and pepper. Stir with a whisk to dissolve. Add the oils and stir to an emulsion. It will keep well in the refrigerator for up to a week.
MAKES ABOUT 400 ML

FRANCK'S BASIL DRESSING

'This is basically the same as the vinaigrette, but made in a blender. It's delicious with any salad, cold meats, cold fish and cold or hot chicken. Of course, because I love bread, I think that that makes the best accompaniment: just pour a little onto the plate and dunk in the bread.'

75 ml white or red wine vinegar

15 ml Dijon mustard

120 ml sunflower oil

200 ml olive oil

15 whole fresh basil leaves

salt and freshly ground black
 pepper to taste

Pour the vinegar and mustard into the blender. At a low speed, add the oils. Once it is emulsified, throw in the basil leaves and the sauce will turn green. While the blender is still going, season with salt and pepper. MAKES ABOUT 400 ML

BEURRE BATTU AUX HERBETTES

(EMULSIFIED HERB BUTTER)

'This is one of those sauces you can serve with anything, because it has such easy-going flavours – pour it over steamed or poached vegetables, fish, chicken or red meat.

100 ml cream

15 ml lemon juice

15 ml Dijon mustard

pinch of chilli powder or
 cayenne pepper

200 g butter, cut into cubes

15 ml chopped fresh parsley

15 ml chopped fresh basil

15 ml chopped fresh tarragon
 (if not available use a pinch
 of dry tarragon)

15 ml snipped chives

15 ml chopped spring onions

salt to taste

Combine the cream, lemon juice, mustard and chilli powder in a small saucepan. Bring to the boil and reduce by half. Whisk in the butter, and stir until almost boiling.
 Blend in a blender, while the butter is hot, for 30 seconds. Return to the saucepan, add the remaining ingredients and serve.
SERVES 4

FRANCK'S PURÉE D'AUBERGINE

(AUBERGINE PURÉE)

'This is a typical Provençal purée to be served with fish or chicken and an acidic sauce. It also makes an excellent spread for my favourite food: good bread.'

1 large aubergine

30 ml water

40 ml butter

1 sprig fresh thyme

salt and freshly ground black
 pepper to taste

2 small garlic cloves, finely
 chopped

Peel and cube the aubergine. Place in a small saucepan with the water and butter, cover and cook gently until the aubergine is meltingly soft. Remove the lid and cook until all the water has evaporated. Add the thyme and the seasoning. While still hot, place in a blender and add the garlic. Blend until smooth. SERVES 4

FRANCK'S L'OLIVADE POUR LES CRUDITÉS

(OLIVE AND TOMATO DIP FOR CRUDITÉS)

'At La Colombe you'll always find this on the table. In my opinion, crudites are the perfect mise en bouche – "a mouth primer". Before you eat, or when you have your first sip of crisp dry wine, you also need crispy veggies with a tangy sauce.

'In summer, when we have all these wonderful vegetables, I offer this as a first course.'

6 very ripe medium tomatoes,
    peeled
250 g pitted green olives,
    drained
15–20 fresh basil leaves
45 ml red wine vinegar
200 ml olive oil
salt and freshly ground black
    pepper to taste

Combine all the ingredients and blend until almost smooth. MAKES 1 LITRE

BREADS AND PASTRIES

'Bread is one of the most magical, rewarding and easiest things to bake. While sailing in the Caribbean, I discovered hunger – and how freshly made bread truly can fill the gap.'

LES PETITS PAINS CAMPAILLOU

'Frank and I discovered this recipe together. We've made wonderful breads together – and revolting breads as well. Frank uses the dough to make long rolls, while at La Colombe we use it to make little rolls in a wood oven. I like what the very violent heat, the leaping flames and the smoke does to the wet dough.

'Campaillou means small, little breads or small country rolls. If you cut the rolls very small they'll cook in 8–10 minutes in a wood-fired oven.

1 kg flour
20 g salt
25 g fresh yeast or 1 sachet
    (10 g) of instant yeast
750 ml lukewarm water

To make the dough, you need a mixer. You simply cannot do it without one, as your arms will get too tired (or you need a very strong wife or husband to take over after a while). The dough is worked for 30–45 minutes at a low speed – this is what releases the gluten and gives the bread its wonderful, elastic and salty taste.

In a large bowl, combine all the ingredients, pouring in the water last. Don't use the dough hook in your mixer – use the K-beater (it looks like a hand and grabs more dough than the hook).

After 30 minutes, take the beater out and put a wet cloth over the dough to let it prove. On a warm day this will take about 40–60 minutes. You don't need to knock it back.

Preheat the oven to 220 °C.

Sprinkle flour on the work surface and turn out the wet dough onto the flour. Use a metal scraper or a large knife to cut the dough into small rolls. Sprinkle more flour on top of each roll.

Prepare the baking tray by sprinkling it with a little flour. Place the rolls on the tray next to one another. When the pan is full, bake for 20–25 minutes. MAKES 3 LOAVES OR 20 ROLLS

MICHETTE À L'HUILE

(OIL BREAD)

Make the same dough as the Les Petits Pains Campaillou. Don't work it as much, though – about 15 minutes is enough.

Generously oil each baking tray. With your hands still full of oil, divide the dough between the two trays. The secret is to let the dough relax in the pan for about 20 minutes.

With oiled hands, stretch the dough to fit the shape of the trays.

Top with any flavours: sliced onions, tomatoes, peppers or garlic, basil, rosemary ... anything you like.

Allow the dough to prove for 45 minutes at room temperature.

Bake at 220 °C for 20–25 minutes.

FILLS 2 STANDARD
BAKING TRAYS

FRANCK'S
PUFF PASTRY

'Either you're into this kind of thing or you're not. I love it – it's like spending all day working at a puzzle, and the result is light and gorgeous.

'If you really don't feel like doing it, buy the pastry. But be warned – the bought version has a blend of margarine and butter and lasts longer and survives heat better. With 100% butter-made puff pastry, the taste is rich and luxurious.'

450 g cake flour, sieved
5 ml salt
450 g butter, softened slightly
180 ml water
10 ml lemon juice or white wine
  vinegar

Sift the flour into a circle on your work surface. Make a well in the middle and put into this the salt, 60 g of the butter, the water and the lemon juice. Mix and knead until the dough is smooth and elastic. Roll the dough into a ball and use a knife to score a cross across the top – to divide the pastry.

Cover the dough with a cloth and leave it to rest in a cool place for about 1 hour.

On a lightly floured surface, roll the dough into a 20-cm square, rolling the corners slightly more thinly than the centre.

Place the remaining butter in a block in the centre of the dough. Bring up the four corners of the pastry over the butter to make an envelope.

Roll this out into a rectangle measuring 25 x 15 cm, then fold in three. Turn this folded rectangle by 90 degrees. This is your first 'fold'. Roll out again to a rectangle the same size as before, and fold in three again, as before. Again turn the pastry by 90 degrees in the same direction as before. This is your second 'fold'.

Cover the dough and refrigerate for 1 hour.

Repeat the process for a third and fourth 'fold', then refrigerate for another hour.

Repeat once more for a fifth and sixth 'fold', then refrigerate for another hour.

MAKES ABOUT 1.1 KG

LA CROÛTE VERTE

(HERB CRUST)

800 g white breadcrumbs (the
  bought variety)
400 g Gruyère or Danish/Italian
  fontina, grated
250 g chopped fresh parsley
a pinch of fresh thyme
600 g butter, softened

Combine all the ingredients in a food processor and work until smooth. Roll out into a thick sausage and wrap up in plastic wrap. It will keep in the fridge for up to 1 week or in the freezer for up to 1 month.

Use on tomatoes or aubergines, halved and baked in the oven, or on baked potatoes and fish.

MAKES ABOUT 1 KG

PASTA DOUGH

'Making pasta is exhausting, but it's a wonderful, therapeutic thing to do. Invest in a small pasta machine – it costs nothing for what it'll do for you and your tastebuds.'

1 kg flour

10 ml salt

7–10 eggs

lots of elbow grease and a
    pasta machine

Sift together the flour and salt. Make a well in the flour and pour in the eggs. Make sure there're no shells. Mix it in with your hands, gradually increasing the circle while you gather more flour from the outside of the well.

You can then make whatever pasta you want – lasagne, fettucine, ravioli moulds, half moons, etc. The rolled dough will have a marvellous silken texture.

MAKES 1.5 KG

CRÊPE BATTER

This is a basic, versatile batter that can be used for both savoury and sweet crêpe dishes.

If the crêpes are intended for a dessert, use butter rather than olive oil. If you wish, a portion of the flour can be replaced with whole-wheat flour.

3 medium eggs

250 ml milk

125 ml water

2.5 ml salt

250 ml flour

30–45 ml olive oil or
    melted butter

Place all ingredients in a blender and blend until smooth. Pour the batter into a bowl, cover and allow to rest at least 1 hour before using.

To cook the crêpes, heat a crêpe pan with a little olive oil or butter. Pour in just enough batter to cover the base of the pan and cook until golden. Turn the crêpe over and cook until brown.

Stack the finished crêpes on top of one another. If they are not to be used right away, wrap them in plastic and refrigerate.

MAKES 12 CRÊPES

INDEX